JEREMIAH & LAMENTATIONS

Judgment and Grace

John MacArthur

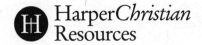
Harper*Christian* Resources

MacArthur Bible Studies
Jeremiah and Lamentations: Judgment and Grace
© 2024 by John MacArthur

Published in Grand Rapids, Michigan, by HarperChristian Resources. HarperChristian Resources is a registered trademark of HarperCollins Christian Publishing, Inc.

Requests for information should be sent to customercare@harpercollins.com.

ISBN 978-0-310-12382-8 (softcover)
ISBN 978-0-310-12383-5 (ebook)

HarperChristian Resources titles may be purchased in bulk for church, business, fundraising, or ministry use. For information, please e-mail ResourceSpecialist@ChurchSource.com.

"Unleashing God's Truth, One Verse at a Time ®" is a trademark of Grace to You. All rights reserved.

Some material from the Introduction, "Keys to the Text," and "Exploring the Meaning" sections are taken from *The MacArthur Bible Commentary*, John MacArthur. Copyright © 2005 Thomas Nelson Publishers.

First Printing February 2024 / Printed in the United States of America

24 25 26 27 28 LBC 5 4 3 2 1

CONTENTS

INTRODUCTION

The prophet Jeremiah was like a lighthouse set in the midst of God's people. The Lord said of him, "Behold, I have made you this day a fortified city and an iron pillar, and bronze walls against the whole land" (Jeremiah 1:18). Jeremiah ministered during the waning decades of Judah and Jerusalem, standing strong against waves of persecution, suffering, rebuke, false teaching, physical deprivation, and isolation. Yet even as those waves crashed against him, the prophet was faithful to declare and display God's warnings to His people for more than fifty years.

Jeremiah's message to the people of Judah was primarily focused on their imminent judgment. Because they had rebelled against God through constant idolatry, child sacrifice, and injustice of all kinds, God's wrath would come against them in the form of an invading army. Jeremiah rightly prophesied not only the military conquest of Judah, including the horrors of the siege, but also the ruin of Jerusalem—even the destruction of Solomon's temple.

Still, even as Jeremiah described the short-term consequences of Judah's rebellion against the Lord, he also spoke of God's long-term plan to provide salvation for all people. Indeed, it was Jeremiah who received this incredible picture of God's future grace: "Behold, the days are coming, says the LORD, when I will make a new covenant with the house of Israel and with the house of Judah. . . . But this is the covenant that I will make with the house of Israel after those days, says the LORD: I will put My law in their minds, and write it on their hearts; and I will be their God, and they shall be My people" (31:31, 33).

THE BOOK OF JEREMIAH

The book gains its title from the human author, who begins with "the words of Jeremiah" (1:1). Jeremiah recounts more of his own life than any other prophet, telling about his ministry, the reactions of his audiences, his testings, and his personal feelings. His name means "Jehovah throws," in the sense of laying down a foundation, or "Jehovah establishes, appoints, or sends."

Seven other Jeremiahs appear in Scripture (see 2 Kings 23:31; 1 Chronicles 5:24; 12:4, 10, 13; Nehemiah 10:2; 12:1), and Jeremiah the prophet is named at least nine times outside of his book (see 2 Chronicles 35:25; 36:12; 36:21, 22; Ezra 1:1; Daniel 9:2; Matthew 2:17; 16:14; 27:9). The authors of the Old and New Testaments quote Jeremiah at least seven times: (1) Daniel 9:2 (see Jeremiah 25:11–12; 29:10); (2) Matthew 2:17–18 (see Jeremiah 31:15); (3) Matthew 27:9 (see Jeremiah 18:2; 19:2, 11; 32:6–9); (4) 1 Corinthians 1:31 (see Jeremiah 9:24); (5) 2 Corinthians 10:17 (see Jeremiah 9:24); (6) Hebrews 8:8–12 (see Jeremiah 31:31–34); and (7) Hebrews 10:16–17 (see Jeremiah 31:33–34).

AUTHOR AND DATE

Jeremiah, who served as both a priest and a prophet, was the son of a priest named Hilkiah (though not the high priest recorded in 2 Kings 22:8 who discovered the Book of the Law). Jeremiah was from the small village of Anathoth (see Jeremiah 1:1), today called Anata, located about three miles northeast of Jerusalem in Benjamin's tribal inheritance. As an object lesson to Judah, Jeremiah remained unmarried (see 16:1–4). He was assisted in ministry by a scribe named Baruch. Jeremiah dictated his words from God to Baruch, who copied them and had custody over the writings compiled from the prophet's messages (see 36:4, 32; 45:1).

Jeremiah has been known as "the weeping prophet" (see 9:1; 13:17; 14:17), living a life of conflict because of his predictions about judgment by the invading Babylonians. He was threatened, tried for his life, put in stocks, forced to flee from King Jehoiakim, publicly humiliated by a false prophet, and thrown into a pit. Jeremiah carried out a ministry directed mostly to his own people in Judah, but which expanded to other nations at times. He appealed to his countrymen to repent and avoid God's judgment via an invader (see chapters 7; 26). Once invasion was certain after Judah refused to repent, he pled with them not to resist the Babylonian conqueror in order to prevent total destruction (see chapter 27). He also called on delegates of other nations to heed his counsel and submit to

Babylon (see chapter 27), and he predicted judgments from God on various nations (see 25:12–38; chapters 46–51).

The dates of Jeremiah's ministry, which spanned five decades, are from the Judean king Josiah's thirteenth year, noted in Jeremiah 1:2 (627 BC), to beyond the fall of Jerusalem to Babylon in 586 BC. After 586 BC, Jeremiah was forced to go with a fleeing remnant of Judah to Egypt (see Jeremiah 43–44). He was possibly still ministering in 570 BC. A rabbinic note claims that when Babylon invaded Egypt in 568/67 BC, Jeremiah was taken captive to Babylon. He could have lived even to pen the book's closing scene c. 561 BC in Babylon, when Judah's king Jehoiachin, captive in Babylon since 597 BC, was allowed liberties in his last days (see 52:31–34). Jeremiah, if still alive at that time, was between eighty-five and ninety years old.

BACKGROUND AND SETTING

Background details of Jeremiah's times are portrayed in 2 Kings 22–25 and 2 Chronicles 34–36. Jeremiah's messages paint pictures of: (1) his people's sin; (2) the invader God would send; (3) the rigors of the siege; and (4) calamities of destruction. Jeremiah's message of impending judgment for idolatry and other sins was preached over a period of forty years (c. 627–586 BC and beyond). His prophecy took place during the reigns of Judah's final five kings: (1) Josiah (640–609 BC), (2) Jehoahaz (609 BC), (3) Jehoiakim (609–598 BC), (4) Jehoiachin (598–597 BC), and (5) Zedekiah (597–586 BC).

The spiritual condition of Judah was one of flagrant idol worship (see Jeremiah 2). King Ahaz, preceding his son Hezekiah long before Jeremiah in Isaiah's day, had set up a system of sacrificing children to the god Molech in the Valley of Hinnom just outside Jerusalem (735–715 BC). Hezekiah led in reforms and cleanup (see Isaiah 36:7), but his son Manasseh continued to foster child sacrifice along with gross idolatry, which continued into Jeremiah's time (see Jeremiah 7:31; 19:5; 32:35). Many people also worshiped the "queen of heaven" (see 7:18; 44:19). Josiah's reforms, reaching their apex in 622 BC, repressed the worst practices outwardly, but the deadly cancer of sin was deep and flourished quickly again after a shallow revival. Religious insincerity, dishonesty, adultery, injustice, tyranny against the helpless, and slander prevailed as the norm, not the exception.

Politically momentous events occurred during Jeremiah's day. Assyria saw its power gradually wane, and then Ashurbanipal (generally regarded as the last great king of the empire) died in 626 BC. Assyria grew so feeble that in 612 BC, her once-seemingly invincible capital, Nineveh, was destroyed by a combined force of Medes and Babylonians (see the book of Nahum). The Neo-Babylonian Empire under Nabopolassar (625–605 BC) became dominant militarily, with victories against Assyria (612 BC), Egypt (609–605 BC), and Israel in three phases (605 BC, as in Daniel 1; 597 BC, as in 2 Kings 24:10–16; and 586 BC, as in Jeremiah 39; 40; 52).

While Joel and Micah had earlier prophesied of Judah's coming judgment, during Josiah's reign God's leading prophets were Jeremiah, Habakkuk, and Zephaniah. Later, Jeremiah's contemporaries, Ezekiel and Daniel, played prominent prophetic roles.

HISTORICAL AND THEOLOGICAL THEMES

The main theme of Jeremiah is judgment upon Judah (chapters 1–29) with future restoration in the messianic kingdom (Jeremiah 23:3–8; 30–33). Whereas Isaiah devoted many chapters to a future glory for Israel (see Isaiah 40–66), Jeremiah gave far less space to this subject. Since God's judgment was imminent, Jeremiah concentrated on current problems as he sought to turn the nation back from the point of no return.

A secondary theme of the book is God's willingness to spare and bless the nation of Judah only if the people repented. Although this is a frequent emphasis, it is most graphically portrayed at the potter's shop (see Jeremiah 18:1–11). A further focus is God's plan for Jeremiah's life, both in his proclamation of God's message and in his commitment to fulfill all of God's will (see 1:5–19; 15:19–21).

Other themes include: (1) God's longing for Israel to be tender toward Him, as in the days of first love (see 2:1–3); (2) Jeremiah's servant tears, as "the weeping prophet" (see 9:1; 14:17); (3) the close, intimate relationship that God had with Israel that He yearned to keep (see 13:11); (4) suffering, as in Jeremiah's trials (see 11:18–23; 20:1–18), and God's sufficiency in all trouble (see 20:11–13); (5) the vital role that God's Word can play in life (see 15:16); (6) the place of faith in expecting restoration from the God for whom nothing is too difficult (see Jeremiah 32, especially verses 17, 27); and (7) prayer for the coordination of God's will with God's action in restoring Israel to its land (see 33:3, 6–18).

INTERPRETIVE CHALLENGES

A number of interpretive questions arise. First, how can one explain why God forbade prayer for the Jews (see 7:16) and God saying that even Moses' and

Samuel's advocacy could not avert judgment (see 15:1)? Second, did Jeremiah make an actual trek of several hundred miles to the Euphrates River, or did he bury his loincloth nearby (see 13:4–7)? Third, how could Jeremiah utter such severe things about the man who announced his birth (see 20:14–18)? Fourth, does the curse on Jeconiah's kingly line relate to Christ (see 22:30)? Fifth, how is one to interpret the promises of Israel's return to its ancient land (see chapters 30–33)? Sixth, how will God fulfill the New Covenant in relation to Israel and the church (see 31:31–34)? The answers to these issues will be included in the study notes at the appropriate passages.

A frequent challenge in the book of Jeremiah is to understand the prophet's messages in their right time setting. The book of Jeremiah is not always arranged chronologically, but often loosely arranged, moving back and forth in time for thematic effect. Ezekiel, by contrast, usually placed his material in chronological order.

THE BOOK OF LAMENTATIONS

Lamentations, which conveys the idea of "loud cries," was derived from a translation of the title as found in the Latin Vulgate and the Septuagint. The Hebrew exclamation "How!" (which expresses "dismay"; see 1:1; 2:1; 4:1) gives the book its Hebrew title. However, the rabbis began to call the book "loud cries" or "lamentations" early on (see Jeremiah 7:29). No other entire Old Testament book contains only laments, as does this distressful dirge, marking the funeral of the once-beautiful city of Jerusalem (see Lamentations 2:15). This book keeps alive the memory of that city's fall (586 BC) and teaches all believers how to deal with suffering.

AUTHOR AND DATE

The author of Lamentations is not named within the book, but there are internal and historical indications that it was Jeremiah. For example, the Septuagint introduces Lamentations 1:1 in this way: "And it came to pass, after Israel had been carried away captive . . . Jeremiah sat weeping . . . lamented . . . and said" (see also 3:48–49). Elsewhere, God told Jeremiah to have Judah lament (see Jeremiah 7:29). Jeremiah also wrote laments for Josiah (see 2 Chronicles 35:25).

Jeremiah wrote Lamentations as an eyewitness (see Lamentations 1:13–15; 2:6, 9; 4:1–12), possibly with Baruch's secretarial help (see Jeremiah 36:4; 45:1), during or soon after Jerusalem's fall in 586 BC. It was mid-July when the city fell and mid-August when the temple was burned. Likely, Jeremiah saw the destruction of the walls, towers, homes, palace, and temple. He wrote while the event remained painfully fresh in his memory but before his forced departure to Egypt c. 583 BC (see Jeremiah 43:1–7).

The language used in Lamentations closely parallels that used by Jeremiah in his much larger prophetic book. Compare, for example: (1) Lamentations 1:2 with Jeremiah 30:14; (2) Lamentations 1:15 with Jeremiah 8:21; (3) Lamentations 1:6 and 2:11 with Jeremiah 9:1, 18; (4) Lamentations 2:22 with Jeremiah 6:25; and (5) Lamentations 4:21 with Jeremiah 49:12.

BACKGROUND AND SETTING

The prophetic seeds of Jerusalem's destruction had already been sown by Joshua, some 800 years earlier (see Joshua 23:15–16). Now, for more than forty years, Jeremiah had prophesied of coming judgment and been scorned by the people for preaching doom (c. 645–605 BC). When that judgment came on the disbelieving people in the form of Nebuchadnezzar and the Babylonian army, Jeremiah still responded with great sorrow and compassion toward his suffering and obstinate people. Lamentations relates closely to the book of Jeremiah, describing his anguish over Jerusalem being judged by God for unrepentant sins.

In the book that bears his name, Jeremiah had predicted this calamity in chapters 1–29. In Lamentations, he concentrates in more detail on the bitter suffering and heartbreak that was experienced in Jerusalem's devastation (see also Psalm 46:4–5). So important was Jerusalem's destruction that the facts are recorded in four separate Old Testament chapters: 2 Kings 25; Jeremiah 39:1–11; Jeremiah 52; and 2 Chronicles 36:11–21.

All 154 verses of Lamentations have been recognized by the Jews as a part of their sacred canon. Along with Ruth, Esther, Song of Solomon, and Ecclesiastes, Lamentations is included among the Old Testament books of the Megilloth, or "five scrolls," which were read in the synagogue on special occasions. Lamentations is read on the ninth of Ab (July/August) to remember the date of Jerusalem's destruction by Nebuchadnezzar. Interestingly, this same date later marked the destruction of Herod's temple by the Romans in AD 70.

HISTORICAL AND THEOLOGICAL THEMES

The chief focus of Lamentations is on God's judgment in response to Judah's sin. This theme can be traced throughout the book (see 1:5, 8, 18, 20; 3:42; 4:6, 13,

22; 5:16). A second theme is the hope found in God's compassion (as in 3:22–24, 31–33; see also Psalm 30:3–5). Although the book deals with disgrace, it turns to God's great faithfulness (see Lamentations 3:22–25) and closes with grace as Jeremiah moves from lamentation to consolation (see 5:19–22).

God's sovereign judgment represents a third current in the book. His holiness was so offended by Judah's sin that He ultimately brought the destructive calamity. Babylon was chosen to be His human instrument of wrath (see 1:5, 12, 15; 2:1, 17; 3:37–38; see also Jeremiah 50:23). Jeremiah mentions Babylon more than 150 times from Jeremiah 20:4 to 52:34, but in Lamentations he never once explicitly names Babylon or its king, Nebuchadnezzar. Only the Lord is identified as the One who dealt with Judah's sin.

Fourth, because the sweeping judgment seemed to be the end of every hope for Israel's salvation and the fulfillment of God's promises (see Lamentations 3:18), much of the book appears in the mode of prayer: (1) Lamentations 1:11, which represents a wailing confession of sin (see also verse 18); (2) Lamentations 3:8, with its anguish when God "shuts out my prayer" (see also 3:43–54; Jeremiah 7:16); (3) Lamentations 3:55–59, where Jeremiah cries to God for relief; (4) Lamentations 3:60–66, where he seeks for recompense to the enemies (which Jeremiah 50–51 guarantees); and (5) Lamentations 5:1–22, with its appeal to heaven for restored mercy (which Jeremiah 30–33 assures) based on the confidence that God is faithful (see Lamentations 3:23).

A fifth feature relates to Christ. Jeremiah's tears (see 3:48–49) compare with Jesus' weeping over the same city of Jerusalem (see Matthew 23:37–39; Luke 19:41–44). Although God was the judge and executioner, it was a grief to Him to bring this destruction. The statement, "In all their affliction, He [God] was afflicted" (Isaiah 63:9), was true in principle. God will one day wipe away all tears (see Isaiah 25:8; Revelation 7:17; 21:4) when sin shall be no more.

An implied warning to all who read this book encompasses a sixth major idea. If God did not hesitate to judge His beloved people (see Deuteronomy 32:10), what will He do to the nations of the world who reject His Word?

INTERPRETIVE CHALLENGES

Certain details pose initial difficulties. Among them are: (1) imprecatory prayers for judgment on other sinners (see Lamentations 1:21–22; 3:64–66); (2) the reason for God shutting out prayer (see 3:8); and (3) the necessity of judgment that is so severe (see 1:1, 14; 3:8).

In the first four chapters, each verse begins in an acrostic pattern—that is, using the twenty-two letters of the Hebrew alphabet in sequence. Chapters 1, 2, and 4 have twenty-two verses corresponding to twenty-two letters, while chapter 3 employs each letter for three consecutive verses until there are twenty-two trios, or sixty-six verses. Chapter 5 is not written alphabetically, though it simulates the pattern in that it has twenty-two verses. An acrostic order, such as in Psalm 119 (where all twenty-two Hebrew letters are used in series of eight verses each), was used to aid memorization. The structure of the book ascends to and then descends from the great confession in Lamentations 3:22–24, "Great is Your faithfulness," which is the literary center of the book.

THE CALL OF JEREMIAH

Jeremiah 1:1–5:31

DRAWING NEAR

How would you describe your calling in life? What skills and gifts has God given you to accomplish this calling?

_____

_____

_____

_____

_____

_____

_____

_____

_____

_____

_____

_____

_____

THE CONTEXT

Many people wonder about their direction in life. They ask questions such as, "What am I here for?" "What is my purpose?" "How can I find purpose and meaning?" Jeremiah did not have to ask such questions. At an early age, God set him apart as a prophet, declaring how he was called to live and what he was to achieve. For example, God said, "Before I formed you in the womb I knew you; before you were born I sanctified you; I ordained you a prophet to the nations" (1:5). And later, "See, I have this day set you over the nations and over the kingdoms, to root out and to pull down, to destroy and to throw down, to build and to plant" (verse 10).

What did it mean to be a prophet in Jeremiah's day? First and foremost, prophets were called to declare the words of God to His people—to say whatever God commanded them to say whenever God commanded them to say it. (They were also called to do what God commanded them to do, as seen in the fact that many of Jeremiah's messages were communicated through object lessons.) Prophets were responsible to confront individuals or entire nations with God's messages. They played an important role as liaisons between God and His people, with leaders or individuals often asking them to inquire of God on their behalf.

The early chapters of Jeremiah offer details on the young prophet's call and God-given assignment. They also explore God's "case" against the people of Judah and Jerusalem—the record of their rebellion and idolatry. Other themes include a call for repentance, Jeremiah's lamentation over the future destruction of Jerusalem, and affirmations of God's justice.

KEYS TO THE TEXT

Read Jeremiah 1:1–5:31, noting the key words and phrases indicated below.

> *THE PREPARATION OF AND CHARGE TO JEREMIAH: Jeremiah's ministry spanned at least five decades—from Judah's king Josiah, in Jeremiah's thirteenth year (627 BC), to the final king of Judah, Zedekiah, in his last year (586 BC).*

1:1. ANATHOTH: A town in the territory of Benjamin, three miles north of Jerusalem, assigned to the Levites (see Joshua 21:18), and the place where Abiathar had once lived (see 1 Kings 2:26).

2. WORD: This term (also used in 5:14; 13:8; 21:11; 24:4; 32:8; 40:1; 50:1) is derived from the verb "to speak" (Hebrew *dabar*) and signifies the word or thing spoken. The phrase "word of the LORD" was used by the prophets at the beginning of a divine message (see 1:13). In the case of prophetic literature, "word" can be a technical term for a prophecy. In the Bible, the word of revelation is associated with prophets (see 26:5), just as wisdom is associated with wise men and the law with priests (see 18:18). Jeremiah used *dabar* more than any other prophet to clarify the authority given to him by God.

3. FIFTH MONTH: Babylonian conquerors began deporting Judeans into captivity in the Hebrew month Ab (July–August) in 586 BC (see Jeremiah 52:12; 2 Kings 25:8–11), shortly after entering Jerusalem on the fourth month and ninth day (see Jeremiah 39:2; 52:6).

5. BEFORE I FORMED YOU: This is not reincarnation; it is God's all-knowing cognizance of Jeremiah and sovereign plan for him before he was conceived (see Paul's similar realization in Galatians 1:15).

6. A YOUTH: Jeremiah's response points out his inability and his inexperience. If as a young man he was twenty to twenty-five years old in 626 BC, he was sixty to sixty-five in 586 BC when Jerusalem fell (see Jeremiah 39), and eighty-five to ninety if he lived to the time of the events depicted in Jeremiah 52:31–34 (c. 561 BC).

7–10. I AM WITH YOU: The power backing Jeremiah's service was God's presence and provision (see 2 Corinthians 3:5).

9. MY WORDS IN YOUR MOUTH: God used Jeremiah as His mouthpiece, speaking His message (see 15:19); thus, his fitting response was to receive God's Word (see 15:16).

10. SET YOU OVER: Because God spoke through Jeremiah, the message has divine authority.

11–16. WHAT DO YOU SEE: Illustrations of God's charge were twofold. First, there was the sign of the almond rod. The almond tree was literally "the wakeful tree," because it awakened from the sleep of winter earlier than the other trees, blooming in January. It was a symbol of God's early judgment, as Jeremiah announced (605–586 BC). Second, the boiling cauldron pictured the Babylonian invaders bringing judgment on Judah (see 20:4).

17–19. SPEAK TO THEM: Jeremiah's part involved proclamation as God's mouthpiece (see verse 17); God's part was preservation in defending the prophet (see verses 18–19). God did protect him often (see 11:18–23; 20:1ff.; 38:7–13).

JEREMIAH'S FIRST MESSAGE: Jeremiah states God's charge against Judah through a series of messages. His first message (2:1–3:5) begins with him pointing to the sensitivity of the Lord and His care for the people of Judah in their early history.

2:1–3. JERUSALEM ... ISRAEL: After centuries, many of the people were now: (1) far from God, whom they had forsaken (see verses 5, 31); (2) deep in idolatry (see verses 11, 27–28); and (3) without true salvation (see verse 8; 5:10a).

3. FIRSTFRUITS: Israel was first to worship the true God (see Exodus 19:5–6) through His covenant with Abraham (see Genesis 12:1–3), which also assured His intent to bless peoples from all nations (see Jeremiah 16:19–21; Daniel 7:27).

8. PRIESTS . . . PROPHETS: Leaders who did not know the Lord set the idolatrous pattern for others (see Hosea 4:6).

13. TWO EVILS: First, Israel had abandoned the Lord, the source of spiritual salvation and sustenance (see Jeremiah 17:8; Psalm 36:9; John 4:14). Second, Israel turned to idolatrous objects of trust; Jeremiah compared these with underground water-storage devices for rainwater, which were broken and let water seep out, thus proving useless.

14. IS ISRAEL A SERVANT: The people needed to ponder this question: "How is it that a people under God's special care are left at the mercy of an enemy, like a worthless slave?"

15. YOUNG LIONS: The figure represents invading soldiers who burned cities (see Jeremiah 4:7); perhaps this is a reference to the disaster from the Babylonians during Jehoiakim's fourth year, and again three years later when he relied on Egypt (see 20:4; 46:2; 2 Kings 24:1–2).

16. NOPH . . . TAHPANHES: These two cities in Egypt stood for the country itself.

18. EGYPT . . . ASSYRIA: Dependence on alliances with Egypt and Assyria was part of Judah's national undoing, a source of shame (see verses 36–37).

SIHOR: This refers to the Nile River.

19. BACKSLIDINGS: This term is often used by the prophets (see Isaiah 57:17; Jeremiah 3:6, 8, 11–14, 22; 8:5; 31:22; 49:4; Hosea 11:7; 14:4) of apostate unbelievers (see also Proverbs 14:14).

23. THE BAALS: An inclusive term referring collectively to false deities.

23–24. DROMEDARY . . . WILD DONKEY: The nation, in chasing other idols, is depicted as a female camel pursuing its instinct and as a wild donkey in heat sniffing the wind to find a mate, craving to attract others of its kind. Other pictures of Israel are that of a thief, who is ashamed when exposed (see verse 26), and that of a maid or a bride who forgets what beautifies her (see verse 32).

3:1. IF A MAN DIVORCES: Such a man was not to take that woman as his wife again, for this would defile her (see Deuteronomy 24:4) and be a scandal. Jeremiah used this analogy to picture Israel as a harlot in the spiritual realm, with many lovers; that is, nations (see Jeremiah 2:18, 25) and idols (see 2:23–25;

3:2, 6–9). Yet the Lord would graciously receive Israel and/or Judah back as His wife if she would repent (see 3:12–14).

> JEREMIAH'S SECOND MESSAGE: *Jeremiah's second message against Judah (3:6–6:30) begins with him using an analogy of God divorcing Israel for her continual sin of unrepentant adultery that the people were committing in the spiritual realm.*

3:6. BACKSLIDING: See note on Jeremiah 2:19.

8. I HAD PUT HER AWAY AND GIVEN HER A CERTIFICATE OF DIVORCE: Although God hates divorce (see Malachi 2:16), it was permitted in cases of unrepentant adultery (see Matthew 5:32; 19:8–9), as indicated by this analogy. God had divorced Israel but not yet Judah (see Isaiah 50:1). In Ezra 10:3, divorce was the right action of God's people to separate from idolatrous wives.

14. I AM MARRIED TO YOU: God pictured His covenant relationship with Israel as a marriage and pleaded with mercy for Judah to repent and return. He would take her back. In the book of Hosea, the restoration of Gomer (the prophet's unfaithful wife) is also a picture of God taking back His wicked, adulterous people.

15–18. IT SHALL COME TO PASS ... IN THOSE DAYS: When Israel repents (see verses 13–14, 22)—which has not happened, but will in the millennial era of God's restoration that the prophets often describe (see Jeremiah 23:5, 6; 30–33; Ezekiel 36)—God will bring these blessings: (1) shepherds to teach them the truth; (2) His own immediate presence on the throne in Jerusalem, not just the ark of His covenant; (3) allegiance even of Gentile nations; (4) righteousness; (5) genuineness in worship; (6) unity of Israel (north) and Judah (south) into one kingdom; and (7) reestablishment in their own Promised Land.

19. AMONG THE CHILDREN: Here is a reference to adoption into God's family, when the people turn back from idols to acknowledge Him as "Father."

20. A WIFE TREACHEROUSLY DEPARTS: Hosea had earlier used this same imagery (c. 755–710 BC). Thus, God had given the divorce because the spiritual adultery was unrepentant. But when repentance comes, He will take Israel back (see Jeremiah 3:1).

O ... ISRAEL: Since the irretrievable dispersion of Israel in the north (722 BC), Judah alone was left to be called by the name "Israel," as Jeremiah sometimes chose to do (see 3:20–23).

22. HEAL: This term (also used in 6:14; 8:11; 15:18; 17:14; 30:17; 51:8) applies literally to the work of a physician. Occasionally it refers to inanimate objects and can best be translated "repair" (see 1 Kings 18:30). More commonly, the word connotes the idea of restoring to normal, as in 2 Chronicles 7:14, where God promised to restore the land if His people prayed. In the book of Psalms, God is praised for His role in healing disease (see Psalm 103:3), healing the broken-hearted (see Psalm 147:3), and healing the soul by providing salvation (see Psalms 30:2; 107:20). Isaiah declared that the healing of God's people results from the sacrificial wounds of His Son (see Isaiah 53:5–12).

4:3. BREAK UP: Jeremiah appealed for a spiritual turnabout from sinful, wasteful lives. He pictured this as the plowing of ground, formerly hard and unproductive because of weeds, in order to make it useful for sowing (see Matthew 13:18–23).

4. CIRCUMCISE: This surgery (see Genesis 17:10–14) was designed to cut away flesh that could hold disease in its folds and could, therefore, pass the disease on to wives. It was important for the preservation of God's people physically. But it was also a symbol of the need for the heart to be cleansed from sin's deadly disease. The really essential surgery needed to happen on the inside, where God calls for taking away fleshly things that keep the heart from being spiritually devoted to Him and from true faith in Him and His will. Jeremiah later expanded on this theme (see 31:31–34; see also Deuteronomy 10:16; 30:6; Romans 2:29). God selected the reproductive organ as the location of the symbol for man's need for cleansing from sin because it is the instrument most indicative of his depravity, since by it he reproduces generations of sinners.

AN IMMINENT INVASION: Jeremiah prophesizes of a disaster that would come "from the north." This evil is Babylon's army, which would invade from that direction.

7. LION: The "lion" on the prowl fit Babylon because of its conquering power, and Babylon was symbolized by the winged lions guarding its royal court. Babylon is later identified in Jeremiah 20:4. Many details in chapter 4 depict conquering warriors (see verses 7, 13, 29).

10. DECEIVED: Like Habakkuk (see 1:12–17), Jeremiah was horrified at these words of judgment, contrasting the prevailing hope of peace. God is sometimes described as if doing a thing He merely permits, such as allowing false prophets

who delude themselves to also deceive a sinful people into thinking peace would follow (see Jeremiah 6:14; 8:11; 1 Kings 22:21–24). God sees how people insist on their delusions and lets it happen.

14. WASH: Jeremiah continued to appeal for the nation to deal with its sin so that national destruction might be averted (see verse 20) while there was still time to repent (see chapters 7; 26).

22. WISE TO DO EVIL: Israelites were wise in doing evil but were dull in knowing to do good; that is, God's will. Paul, applying the principle but turning it to the positive, wanted the believers in Rome to be wise to do good but unlearned in the skill of doing evil (see Romans 16:19).

23. WITHOUT FORM: Jeremiah may be borrowing the language, but the description, in its context, is not of creation as in Genesis 1:2 but of judgment on the land of Israel and its cities (see verse 20). The invader left it desolate of the previous form and void of inhabitants because of slaying and flight (see verse 25). The heavens gave no light, possibly due to smoke from fires that were destroying cities (see verses 7, 20).

5:1. FIND A MAN: The city was too sinful to have even one man who, by truth and justice, could qualify to be an advocate to secure pardon for Judah. Refusal to repent was the norm (see verse 3) for the common people (see verse 4) and for the leaders (see verse 5).

6. LION: Three animals that tear and eat their victims represented the invader: the lion (see note on 4:6–7), the wolf, and the leopard, all picturing vicious judgment on both poor (see verse 4) and rich (see verse 5).

7. ADULTERY: Often the idea of adultery is figurative of idolatry or political alliances (see note on 3:1), but the language here refers to physical adultery by men seeking out a harlot or going to their neighbors' wives (see verse 8), thus violating the seventh Commandment (see Exodus 20:14).

10. NOT THE LORD'S: The people, depicted as vine branches to be destroyed (see Jeremiah 11:16–17), did not genuinely know the Lord in a saving relationship but had forsaken Him and given allegiance to other gods. The description of having eyes but not seeing and ears but not hearing (see verse 21) is used by Isaiah (see Isaiah 6:9) and Jesus Christ (see Matthew 13:13) for such false professors as these branches. Jesus also referred to false branches in John 15:2, 6 that were burned.

14. MY WORDS ... FIRE: The judgment on Judah prophesied in God's Word by Jeremiah will bring destruction but not elimination (see verse 18) to the nation (see 23:29).

22. SAND . . . OF THE SEA: God's providential acts in the natural world, such as (1) creating the seashore to prevent flooding, (2) giving rain at the appropriate times (see verse 24), and (3) providing time for harvest (see verse 24), are witness to the Lord's reality and grace. As the nation turns away from God, He will take these unappreciated, gracious gifts away (see verse 25).

31. PROPHESY FALSELY: These included prophets with bogus messages, priests who asserted their own authority, and also followers who indulged such misrepresentations. All are guilty before God.

UNLEASHING THE TEXT

1) What stands out about Jeremiah based on these chapters? What are some ways to describe him?

_____

_____

_____

_____

_____

_____

2) Jeremiah 1 includes several images connected to the prophet's call. What do they communicate?

_____

_____

_____

_____

_____

_____

3) Jeremiah 2 highlights some of the depths of Judah's rebellion against God. What were the key roots or foundations of their sin?

_____

_____

_____

_____

_____

_____

4) What are some specific examples of God preparing Jeremiah and the citizens of Jerusalem for the coming invasion from Babylon?

_____

_____

_____

_____

_____

_____

EXPLORING THE MEANING

God prepared Jeremiah for His work. God's prophets in Israel and Judah had an incredibly difficult job. They were commanded to point out how God's people had transgressed His covenant, deliver extremely unpopular messages of imminent judgment, and directly confront both spiritual and political leaders who possessed the power to deliver unpleasant consequences—including the prophet's death. Thankfully, God did not call Jeremiah to his prophetic ministry and leave him to figure things out on his own. Instead, He prepared Jeremiah for the work ahead. This included shaping Jeremiah's character and personality so that he had the inner strength to withstand criticism and rebuke. As God said to him, "Behold, I have made you this day a fortified city and an iron pillar, and bronze walls against the whole land—against the kings of Judah, against its princes, against its priests, and against the people of the land" (1:18). God also prepared Jeremiah for his difficult work by promising (and providing) ongoing strength and support. Jeremiah would be able to weather the storms of criticism and attack because he would not be alone. "'They will fight against you, but they shall not prevail against you. For I am with you,' says the LORD, 'to deliver you'" (1:19).

God prepared Jeremiah with His message. Jeremiah's task was monumental: to confront the people of Judah with the reality of their sin and then call them to repent and return to serving the Lord. What could one man possibly say to an entire nation? How could a young man stand in front of priests and kings and speak with authority? Fortunately, Jeremiah did not have to come up with his message based on his experience, wisdom, or skill. Instead, God appointed Jeremiah as His mouthpiece, declaring His message through His prophet. "Then the LORD put forth His hand and touched my mouth, and the LORD said to me: 'Behold, I have put My words in your mouth'" (1:9). This language is similar to a more vivid experience expressed by the prophet Ezekiel: "Moreover He said to me, 'Son of man, eat what you find; eat this scroll, and go, speak to the house of Israel.' So I opened my mouth, and He caused me to eat that scroll. And He said to me, 'Son of man, feed your belly, and fill your stomach with this scroll that I give you.' So I ate, and it was in my mouth like honey in sweetness" (Ezekiel 3:1–3). In both cases, God provided the message that He desired His prophets to proclaim.

God prepared Jeremiah for His coming wrath. It can be easy to forget that for Jeremiah, declaring a message of judgment against Judah was declaring a message of judgment against himself and his home. Jeremiah was from the small town of Anathoth (see 1:1), located about three miles north of Jerusalem. Therefore, the impending destruction of Judah and Jerusalem was personally painful, yet God prepared him with the reality of that judgment from the beginning. The prophet's second "word of the LORD" included this image: "I see a boiling pot, and it is facing away from the north" (1:13). God explained the meaning behind the vision—that "calamity" would break forth from the "kingdoms of the north" and descend upon the gates of Jerusalem and its walls and all the cities of Judah. Understandably, this message was difficult for Jeremiah to process. "O my soul, my soul!" he declared. "I am pained in my very heart! My heart makes a noise in me; I cannot hold my peace, because you have heard, O my soul, the sound of the trumpet, the alarm of war" (4:19). Yet being forewarned about the coming judgment allowed Jeremiah to process his pain and perform his role for the people of Judah.

REFLECTING ON THE TEXT

5) What challenges do you face today when you take a stand for the truth of God's Word?

_____

_____

_____

_____

_____

_____

6) Christians have unprecedented access to Scripture, but what obstacles often hinder you from making Scripture a key part of your life, as was true of the prophets Jeremiah and Ezekiel?

_____

_____

_____

_____

_____

7) What causes you to feel pain or sorrow about the current state of the world? Why?

_____

_____

_____

_____

_____

8) Followers of Jesus are are called to proclaim the "good news" of the gospel (see Mark 16:15). How would you summarize that good news in your own words?

_____

_____

_____

_____

_____

PERSONAL RESPONSE

9) Are you being faithful to God in your current circumstance? Explain why or why not.

_____

_____

_____

_____

10) How satisfied are you with your current habits and routines when it comes to engaging the Bible? What are some goals you would like to achieve on that front in the coming months?

_____

_____

_____

_____

_____

_____

_____

2

THE CHARGE AGAINST JUDAH
Jeremiah 6:1–11:23

DRAWING NEAR

On a scale of 1 (low) to 10 (high), how comfortable are you with offering critique or criticism to others when it seems needed? Explain your response.

_____

_____

_____

_____

_____

_____

_____

_____

_____

_____

_____

_____

_____

_____

_____

_____

_____

_____

THE CONTEXT

As we saw in the previous lesson, the book of Jeremiah begins with an autobiographical passage that describes the prophet being called by God as a young man. The Lord promised to put His word in Jeremiah's mouth and support him while he carried out his ministry. For his part, Jeremiah was to stand as a strong tower against the rebellion, idolatry, and persecution of those who lived in Judah and Jerusalem. He was to faithfully declare the messages of God. Of course, all of this was no easy task given the antagonism that most prophets experienced whenever they confronted people with truths those people did not want to hear.

In Jeremiah's first message (2:1–3:5), God reflected on His relationship with His people and their rebellion against Him. In Jeremiah's second message (3:6–6:30), God compared the rebellion of Judah with the previous actions of her "sister," Israel, and called them both to repentance. As a reminder, the promised land had been divided after the death of King Solomon, with most of the tribes forming the northern kingdom of Israel, while the tribes of Judah and Benjamin formed the southern kingdom of Judah. In the decades before Jeremiah's ministry, Israel had been swallowed up in captivity by Assyria. Jeremiah's message also included direct promises of an imminent invasion from the north.

In this lesson, we will primarily explore Jeremiah's third message to the people of Judah and Jerusalem, which is recorded in 7:1–10:25. This message was delivered at the gate of the temple in Jerusalem. It includes a catalogue of Israel's idolatry and of the false messages of "peace" being declared by other prophets who were not called by God.

KEYS TO THE TEXT

Read Jeremiah 6:1–11:23, noting the key words and phrases indicated below.

> IMPENDING DESTRUCTION: *Jeremiah concludes his second message against Judah (3:6–6:30) by reiterating an invasion would be coming from the north—in the form of Babylon's army—if the people did not repent and turn from idolatry.*

6:1. TEKOA . . . BETH HACCEREM: Tekoa, the home of Amos, was six miles south of Bethlehem. The location of Beth Haccerem ("vineyard house") is unknown, but probably near Tekoa. As the enemy came from the north, the people would flee south.

NORTH: See note on Jeremiah 4:6–7.

3. SHEPHERDS: The term "shepherd" (also used in 23:4; 31:10; 43:12; 49:19; 50:44; 51:23) refers to someone who feeds and tends domestic animals. David spoke of God as his Shepherd because God provided, sustained, and guided him (see Psalm 23). Kings and other leaders were also seen as shepherds of their people, and the title "shepherd" was frequently applied to kings in the ancient Middle East. David was a true shepherd-king, responsibly leading and protecting his people (see 2 Samuel 5:1–2). Jeremiah rebuked the leaders of Israel who were false shepherds and failed in their responsibility of caring for the spiritual well-being of God's people (see Jeremiah 23:1–4). In this verse, the term "shepherds" refers to the hostile leaders of the invading Babylonians, whose soldiers were compared with flocks.

6. CUT DOWN TREES: A siege tactic is described in which trees were used to build up ramps against the city walls.

9. THOROUGHLY GLEAN: Unlike the benevolent practice of leaving food in the field for the poor to glean (see Leviticus 19:9–10; Ruth 2:5–18), the Babylonians would leave no one when they "harvested" Judah.

14. PEACE, PEACE: Wicked leaders among the prophets and priests (see verse 13) proclaimed peace falsely and gave weak and brief comfort. They provided no true healing from the spiritual wound, not having discernment to deal with the sin and its effects (see verse 15). The need was to return to obedience (see verse 16; see also 8:11; 1 Thessalonians 5:3).

16. ASK FOR THE OLD PATHS: Here is the image of travelers who are lost, stopping to inquire about the right way they once knew before they wandered so far away from it.

17. WATCHMEN: Prophets.

20. NOT ACCEPTABLE: Using imported fragrances in their offerings did not make them acceptable to God when the worshipers rejected His words (see verse 19).

21. STUMBLING BLOCKS: See Isaiah 8:14; Matthew 21:44; 1 Peter 2:8.

22–23. A GREAT NATION WILL BE RAISED: A description of the Babylonians.

27–30. I HAVE SET YOU AS AN ASSAYER AND A FORTRESS: God placed Jeremiah as a kind of assayer to test the people's obedience. He also was a "fortress," meaning a "tester" who works with metals. Their sin prevented them from being pure silver; rather, they were bronze, iron, lead, even impure silver, so that they failed the test.

JEREMIAH'S THIRD MESSAGE: Jeremiah's third message against Judah (7:1–10:25) represents his first temple sermon, proclaimed "in the gate of the LORD's house" (verse 2); another is found in chapter 26. God was aroused against the sins He names, especially at His temple becoming "a den of thieves" (verse 11).

7:1. THE WORD THAT CAME: The point of Jeremiah's third message was that if Israel would repent, even at this late hour, God would still keep the conqueror from coming (see verses 3, 7). They must reject lies such as the false hope that peace is certain, based on the reasoning that the Lord would never bring calamity on His own temple (see verse 4). They must turn from their sins (see verses 3, 5, 9) and end their hypocrisy (see verse 10).

7. THE LAND . . . I GAVE . . . FOREVER: God refers to the unconditional element of the land promise in the Abrahamic covenant (see Genesis 12; 15; 17; 22).

12. GO . . . TO . . . SHILOH: God calls them to return to Shiloh where the tabernacle dwelt along with the ark of the covenant. He permitted the Philistines to devastate that place (see 1 Samuel 4), and He was ready to do similarly with Jerusalem, the place of His temple (see Jeremiah 7:13–14).

13. RISING UP EARLY: This refers to the daily ministry of the prophets (see verse 25).

15. AS I HAVE CAST OUT . . . EPHRAIM: Ephraim represents the northern kingdom of Israel, as it was the leading tribe (see 2 Kings 17:23). As God had exiled them to Assyria (c. 722 BC), even though they were more in number and power, so He would do to the southern kingdom.

16. THEREFORE DO NOT PRAY: God told His spokesman not to pray for the people (see Jeremiah 11:14). He did not find Judah inclined to repent. Instead, He found the glib use of self-deluding slogans, such as in verse 4, and flagrant idol worship in verse 18 from a people insistent on not hearing (see verse 27; 19:15; see also 1 John 5:16).

18. THE QUEEN OF HEAVEN: See Jeremiah 44:17–19, 25. The Jews were worshiping Ishtar, an Assyrian and Babylonian goddess also called Ashtoreth and Astarte, the wife of Baal or Molech. Because these deities symbolized generative power, their worship involved prostitution.

22. I DID NOT . . . COMMAND: Bible writers sometimes use apparent negation to make a comparative emphasis. What God commanded His people at the Exodus was not so much the offerings as it was the heart obedience that prompted

the offerings. See this comparative sense used elsewhere (Deuteronomy 5:3; Hosea 6:6; 1 John 3:18).

22–23. OFFERINGS . . . SACRIFICES . . . OBEY: Here is a crucial emphasis on internal obedience. See Joshua 1:8; 1 Samuel 15:22; Proverbs 15:8; 21:3; Isaiah 1:11–17; Hosea 6:6; Matthew 9:13.

25. RISING UP EARLY: See Jeremiah 7:13.

29. CUT OFF YOUR HAIR: This is a sign depicting God's cutting the nation off and casting them into exile. Ezekiel used a similar illustration by cutting his hair (see Ezekiel 5:1–4). God never casts away the genuinely saved from spiritual salvation (see John 6:37; 10:28–29).

31. BURN THEIR SONS: Although God forbade this atrocity (see Leviticus 18:21; 20:2–5; Deuteronomy 12:31), Israelites still offered babies as sacrifices at the high places of idol worship (Tophet) in the valley of Hinnom (south end of Jerusalem). They offered them to the fire god Molech, under the delusion that this god would reward them. See note on Jeremiah 19:6.

32. VALLEY OF SLAUGHTER: God renamed the place because great carnage would be forthcoming in the Babylonian invasion.

8:1. BRING OUT THE BONES: Conquerors would ransack all the tombs to gain treasures and then humiliate the Jews by scattering the bones of the rich and honored in open spaces as a tribute to the superiority of their gods (see verse 2).

4. NOT RISE . . . NOT RETURN: Jeremiah spoke of the natural instinct of one who falls, to get up, and of one who leaves, to return, but Judah did not possess this instinct.

5. BACKSLIDING: See note on Jeremiah 2:19.

7. STORK . . . TURTLEDOVE . . . SWIFT . . . SWALLOW: The instinct of the migratory birds leads them with unfailing regularity to return every spring from their winter homes. But God's people will not return, though the winter of divine wrath is arriving.

11. PEACE, PEACE: See Jeremiah 4:10; 6:14.

16. DAN: The territory of this tribe was on the northern border of the land where the invasion would begin and sweep south.

17. I WILL SEND SERPENTS AMONG YOU: This is a figurative picture of the Babylonian victors.

19. FAR COUNTRY: This is the cry of the exiled Jews that will come after they are taken captive into Babylon. They will wonder why God would let this happen to His land and people.

20–22. WE ARE NOT SAVED: The coming devastation is compared with the hopeless anguish when harvest time has passed but people are still in desperate need. Jeremiah identified with his people's suffering (see verse 21) as a man of tears (see 9:1) but saw a doom so pronounced that there was no comforting remedy. There was no healing balm, the kind in abundance in Gilead (east of the Sea of Galilee), and no physician to cure (see Genesis 37:25; 43:11).

9:1. WATERS . . . TEARS: Jeremiah cared so greatly that he longed for the relief of flooding tears or a place of retreat to be temporarily free of the burden of Judah's sins.

2. A LODGING PLACE FOR TRAVELERS: Simple square buildings with an open court were built in remote areas to accommodate caravans. Though it would be lonely and filthy in the wilderness, Jeremiah preferred it to Jerusalem in order to be removed from the moral pollution of the people, which he described in Jeremiah 9:3–8.

3. DO NOT KNOW ME: See note on Jeremiah 5:10.

15. WORMWOOD: The Lord pictured the awful suffering of the judgment as wormwood, which had very bitter leaves. Their food would be bitterness, and their water as foul as gall, a poisonous herb.

22. CARCASSES OF MEN: Their carcasses will be trampled contemptuously, as worthless, by the enemy.

24. UNDERSTANDS AND KNOWS ME: Nothing but a true knowledge of God can save the nation. Paul refers to this passage twice (see 1 Corinthians 1:31; 2 Corinthians 10:17).

26. EGYPT . . . WILDERNESS: A preview of God's judgment of the nations, which is detailed in chapters 46–51.

UNCIRCUMCISED . . . HEART: See note on Jeremiah 4:4.

10:2. THE SIGNS OF HEAVEN: Gentiles worshiped celestial bodies, including the sun, moon, and stars.

4. DECORATE: Idols were often carved from wood (see verse 3) and ornamented with gold or silver (see verse 9). Some were molded from clay (see Judges 18:17; Isaiah 42:17). The context points out the impossibility (see verses 3–5) of such nonexistent gods punishing or rewarding humans.

7. KING: God, who sovereignly created and controls all things (see verses 12, 16; Deuteronomy 4:35), is the eternal, living God (see Psalms 47; 145), who alone is worthy of trust. By contrast, earthly idols have to be fashioned by humans (see verse 9) and will perish (see verse 15).

9. TARSHISH: Possibly a commercial port in southern Spain or on the island of Sardinia. See Jonah 1:3.

UPHAZ: The location is uncertain.

11–16. THE GODS: The true and living Creator God is again contrasted with dead idols.

16. PORTION OF JACOB: God is the all-sufficient source for His people (see Numbers 18:20), and He will not fail them as idols do (see Jeremiah 11:12).

ISRAEL IS THE TRIBE OF HIS INHERITANCE: To this nation, God gave His inheritance in covenant love.

20. MY TENT IS PLUNDERED: Jeremiah, using a nomadic metaphor, shifted into words that Israelites will speak when the invaders attack. They will feel "woe" due to their "wound" and cry out over their homes being plundered and their children being killed or scattered to exile.

23. THE WAY . . . IS NOT IN HIMSELF: Man is incapable of guiding his own life adequately. This prayer shifts to his need of God (see Proverbs 3:5–6; 16:9), who had a plan for Jeremiah before he was even born (see Jeremiah 1:5).

24–25. O LORD, CORRECT ME, BUT WITH JUSTICE: Jeremiah saw himself ("correct me") associated with his people (see Daniel 9:1ff.) and understood the nation must be punished, but desired some mercy and moderation; he prayed that God's full fury would be poured on the nations that induced the Jews into idolatry.

JEREMIAH'S FOURTH MESSAGE: Jeremiah begins his fourth message against Judah (11:1–13:27) with a reference to God's covenant, summarized in verses 3–5, which promised curses for disobeying and blessings for obeying (see Deuteronomy 27:26–28:68).

11:4. THE IRON FURNACE: A metaphor for the hardship of Egyptian bondage, hundreds of years earlier (see Exodus 1:8–14).

9. A CONSPIRACY: This refers to a deliberate resisting of God's appeals for repentance and an insistence upon trusting their own "peace" message and idols.

13. CITIES . . . GODS: Judah was so filled with idolatry that there were false deities for every city and a polluted altar on every street.

14. DO NOT PRAY: See note on Jeremiah 7:16. The people's own prayers, as long as they rejected God, could not gain the answer they desired (see verse 11; Psalm 66:18), and the same was true of another's prayers for them.

15. MY BELOVED: A phrase showing God's sensitive regard for His relationship to Israel as a nation (see Jeremiah 2:2; 12:7). It does not carry the assumption, however, that every individual is spiritually saved (see 5:10a).

LEWD DEEDS: Shameful idolatry that defiled all that befits true temple worship, such as the examples in Ezekiel 8:6–13. These were gross violations of the first three commandments (see Exodus 20:2–7).

HOLY FLESH: In some way, they corrupted the animal sacrifices by committing sin, which they enjoyed (see Jeremiah 7:10).

16–17. GREEN OLIVE TREE: Israel was pictured as a grapevine (see 2:21), then an olive tree meant to bear good fruit. However, they produced fruit that calls only for the fire of judgment (as in 5:10).

18–23. YOU SHOWED ME: Jeremiah's fellow townsmen from Anathoth, one of the forty-eight cities throughout the land dedicated to the Levites, plotted his death. Their words, "Let us destroy the tree," indicate their desire to silence Jeremiah by murder.

20. LET ME SEE YOUR VENGEANCE: Jeremiah pleaded for God's defense on his behalf, actually guaranteed in 1:8, 18–19.

UNLEASHING THE TEXT

1) Which elements of Jeremiah's third message to the people of Judah struck you as most compelling or convicting? Why?

_____

_____

_____

_____

_____

_____

2) What are some of the criticims or accusations that God leveled against His people?

_____

_____

_____

_____

_____

_____

3) Look again at Jeremiah 8:4–17. What messages were the false teachers and false prophets proclaiming to the people of Jerusalem?

_____

_____

_____

_____

4) Look also at Jeremiah 10:1–10. What specific criticisms did Jeremiah have for those who worshiped idols?

_____

_____

_____

EXPLORING THE MEANING

The people had the opportunity to repent. One of Jeremiah's roles as a prophet was to prophesy—to declare what God had decreed was going to happen in the future. However, it is important to remember that many of the prophesies God delivered through His servants were conditional. In other words, these things would occur *if* the people receiving those prophecies continued on their current path. This was the case for the people of Judah. Through Jeremiah, God declared the horrors of His imminent judgment and wrath. However, He also made it clear that those horrors could be averted if the people repented and returned to Him. Jeremiah was standing at the gates of the temple when he declared, "Thus says the LORD of hosts, the God of Israel: 'Amend your ways and your doings, and I will cause you to dwell in this place'" (7:3). He later added, "For if you thoroughly amend your ways and your doings . . . then I will cause you to dwell in this place, in the land that I gave to your fathers forever and ever" (verses 5,7). The people of Judah had the chance to repent. But unfortunately, they refused.

The people were listening to false prophets. Why did the people of Judah and Jerusalem refuse to repent when doing so could have spared them from God's wrath? Part of the answer seems to be that Jeremiah was not the only "prophet" operating in the land. Many false prophets ministered throughout

Judah in that day, especially in the city of Jerusalem. Their often-repeated message was that God would never allow a foreign army to invade His city and destroy His temple. Jeremiah cried out against these false teachers: "Do not trust in these lying words, saying, 'The temple of the LORD, the temple of the LORD, the temple of the LORD are these'" (7:4). He appealed to the people's common sense: "Will you steal, murder, commit adultery, swear falsely, burn incense to Baal, and walk after other gods whom you do not know, and then come and stand before Me in this house which is called by My name, and say, 'We are delivered to do all these abominations'?" (7:9–10). Jeremiah also reminded the people that God had not spared Shiloh in the past, which was the location of the tabernacle before Jerusalem became His holy city. "But go now to My place which was in Shiloh, where I set My name at the first, and see what I did to it because of the wickedness of My people Israel" (7:12).

The people were infatuated with idols. Another reason why the people refused to repent is because they were deeply invested in idolatry. Many of the citizens of Judah, having lost hold of their faith in God and His covenants, had turned to the false gods of surrounding nations and cultures. Baal worship was common in that region and had been a powerful snare for the kings of Israel. Many in Israel had also turned to Ashtoreth, also known as "the queen of heaven." She was held to be the wife of Baal or Molech and was connected with fertility. Pagans believed that by worshiping Ashtoreth through sex with temple prostitutes, they could increase the odds of fertility for their families and fields. Most abhorrent was the worship of Molech, the fire god. Pagan priests claimed that child sacrifice—burning babies in ritual fires—would trigger Molech to offer rewards. God specifically spoke against this practice, saying, "They have built the high places of Tophet, which is in the Valley of the Son of Hinnom, to burn their sons and their daughters in the fire, which I did not command, nor did it come into My heart" (7:31).

REFLECTING ON THE TEXT

5) What does it mean to "repent"? What is involved in that process?

_____

_____

_____

_____

6) False teachers are still a problem today, both inside and outside the church. How can you discern whether someone is a false teacher (see 1 Timothy 6:3–5)?

7) Where do you see evidence of idolatry in today's culture? Is it evident in your life? Explain your response.

8) What is the answer for getting rid of idolatry and turning to God? What does that look like on a practical level?

PERSONAL RESPONSE

9) When has the Holy Spirit convicted you to repent of sin in your life? What happened in that situation?

10) What steps can you take to ensure that you are not listening to or supporting false teachers?

_____

_____

_____

_____

_____

_____

_____

_____

3

Parables in Action
Jeremiah 12:1–17:18

Drawing Near

Who are some coaches, teachers, or mentors who have made a significant impact on your life? What did they do that was so helpful to you?

_____

_____

_____

_____

_____

_____

_____

_____

_____

_____

_____

_____

_____

_____

The Context

The book of Jeremiah contains more biographical information about its author than most of the other prophetic books. This information includes many details about Jeremiah's personal life and experiences—including his early call to be a prophet and God's charge "to root out and to pull down, to destroy and to throw down, to build and to plant" (1:10). In chapter 11, the prophet offers another biographical interlude in which God assures him the men of Anathoth (Jeremiah's hometown) who were seeking to kill him would not succeed.

This event—an attempted assassination by people he knew—seems to be the catalyst for a question-and-answer session between Jeremiah and God. It begins in chapter 12 with Jeremiah asking a question that many have pondered over the centuries: "Why does the way of the wicked prosper? Why are those happy who deal so treacherously?" (verse 1). God's answer offered both a picture of His heart and His plans for the future. After reminding Jeremiah to remain steadfast in the face of difficulty, He said, "I have forsaken My house, I have left My heritage; I have given the dearly beloved of My soul into the hand of her enemies" (verse 7).

In this lesson, we will explore several instances in which Jeremiah used object lessons—or was himself used as an object lesson—to illustrate spiritual truths. For example, God commanded Jeremiah to bury an expensive linen sash next to the Euphrates River (a round trip of more than 1,000 miles) in order to illustrate the ways in which Judah's pride would be ruined by its coming destruction at the hands of the Babylonians. These living parables were not offered for sport or for showmanship, but rather as a means of illustrating the truth and capturing the attention of those whom God wanted to reach.

KEYS TO THE TEXT

Read Jeremiah 12:1–17:18, noting the key words and phrases indicated below.

> JEREMIAH'S QUESTION: *Jeremiah continues his fourth message against Judah (11:1–13:27) with a question to God as to why the wicked escape unscathed for a time. This issue has often been raised by God's people (see Psalm 73; Habakkuk 1:2–4).*

12:3. PULL THEM OUT . . . FOR THE SLAUGHTER: The prophet here turned from the sadness of pleading for his people to calling on God to punish them. Such imprecatory prayers are similar to prayers throughout the Psalms.

4. HE WILL NOT SEE OUR FINAL END: Here is the foolish idea that Jeremiah was wrong and didn't know how things would happen.

5. IF YOU HAVE RUN: The Lord replied to Jeremiah, telling him that if he grew faint with lesser trials and felt like quitting, what would he do when the battle got even harder?

FLOODPLAIN OF THE JORDAN: The Jordan River in flood stage overflowed its banks into a plain that grew up as a thicket. The point is that Jeremiah needed to be ready to deal with tougher testings, pictured by the invaders overwhelming the land like a flood, or posing great danger as in the Jordan thicket where concealed wild animals could terrify a person.

6. EVEN YOUR BROTHERS: Jeremiah met antagonism not only from fellow townsmen (see note on 11:18–23) but from his own family! He was separated from them (see verse 7).

8. LIKE A LION: Jeremiah's own people collectively are like a lion acting ferociously against him.

9. A SPECKLED VULTURE: God's people, speckled with sin and compromise, are opposed by other vultures; that is, enemy nations.

12. SWORD OF THE LORD: God's strength can be used for defending (see 47:6; Judges 7:20) or in this case, condemning. The Babylonians were God's sword doing His will.

14. EVIL NEIGHBORS: Other nations that hurt Israel will, in their turn, also receive judgment from the Lord (see Jeremiah 9:26; 25:14–32; chapters 46–51).

15. BRING THEM BACK: God will restore His people to the land of Israel in a future millennial day, as indicated in chapters 30–33.

13:1. A LINEN SASH: One of several signs Jeremiah enacted to illustrate God's message (see Introduction) involved putting a linen sash (generally the inner garment against the skin) around his waist. This depicted Israel's close intimacy with God in the covenant so that they could glorify Him (see verse 11).

DO NOT PUT IT IN WATER: This signified the moral filth of the nation. Buried and allowed time to rot (see verse 7), the sash pictured Israel as useless to God due to sin (see verse 10). Hiding it by the Euphrates River (see verse 6) pointed to the land of Babylon, where God would exile Israel to deal with her pride (see verse 9).

4. EUPHRATES: This refers to a site on the Euphrates River because (1) the Euphrates is the area of the Exile (see Jeremiah 20:4); (2) "many days" fits the round trip of well over 1,000 miles (see verse 6); and (3) the ruining of the nation's pride (see verse 9) relates to judgment by Babylon (see verses 10–11).

12–14. EVERY BOTTLE SHALL BE FILLED WITH WINE: God pictured the inhabitants of Israel during Babylon's invasion as bottles or skins of wine. As wine causes drunkenness, they will be dazed, stumbling in darkness (see verse 16), out of control, and victims of destruction (see verse 14).

16. GIVE GLORY TO THE LORD: This means to show by repentance and obedience to God that the nation respects His majesty.

17. WEEP: This describes the act of wailing, which expresses emotions ranging from grief to happiness. While the word is often associated with lamentation, the "bitter wailing" of ancient people who were mourning their dead (see 2 Samuel 1:12), it is also used with expressions of joy (see Genesis 29:11). The ancients wept when saying farewell (see Ruth 1:9), over impending doom (see Jeremiah 9:1; 31:16), to express their joy over the rebuilt temple (see Ezra 3:12), and at the burial of an individual (see Genesis 50:1). In the book of Lamentations, Jeremiah weeps over the sins of the people—the sins that would eventually result in the destruction of Jerusalem (see Lamentations 1:1, 16).

18. KING . . . QUEEN MOTHER: Jehoiachin and Nehushta, c. 597 BC (see Jeremiah 22:24–26; 29:2; 2 Kings 24:8–17). Because the king was only eighteen years old, she held the real power.

19. WHOLLY CARRIED AWAY: "All" and "wholly" do not require absolutely every individual, for Jeremiah elsewhere explains that some people were to be killed and a remnant would be left in the land or fleeing to Egypt (see chapters 39–44).

23. ETHIOPIAN . . . LEOPARD: The vivid analogy assumes that sinners cannot change their sinful natures ("incurably sick"). Only God can change the heart (see 31:18, 31–34).

26. UNCOVER YOUR SKIRTS OVER YOUR FACE: This was done to shame captive women and prostitutes (see Nahum 3:5).

27. YOUR LUSTFUL NEIGHINGS: This refers to desire at an animal level, without conscience.

> JEREMIAH'S FIFTH MESSAGE: Jeremiah appears to have given the opening chapter of his fifth message (14:1–17:18) during a time of drought in Judah (see verses 2–6).

14:2. AND HER GATES LANGUISH: The gates were the place of public concourse, which during drought and consequent famine were empty or occupied by mourners.

7. O LORD: Jeremiah pursues a series of prayers in which he dialogues with the Lord, who hears and responds (see 1:7; 12:5–17). Five rounds or exchanges occur (14:7–12; 14:13–18; 14:19–15:9; 15:10–14; 15:15–21).

7–9. OUR BACKSLIDINGS: The prophet confessed Judah's guilt but reminds God that His reputation is connected with what happens to His people (see verses 7, 9). Jeremiah asks that the Lord not be indifferent as a foreigner or overnight visitor (see verse 8).

10–12. THUS SAYS THE LORD: God responded in this first exchange that (1) He must judge Judah for chronic sinfulness, (2) Jeremiah is not to pray for the sparing of Judah, and (3) He will not respond to their prayers since unrepentance must be punished (see note on 11:14).

13. THE PROPHETS SAY: Jeremiah seemed to put forth the excuse that the people could not help themselves since the false prophets deluded them with lying assurances of peace.

14–18. PROPHESY LIES IN MY NAME: The excuse was not valid. These were deceits spawned from the prophets' lying hearts. The prophets would suffer for their own sins (see verses 14–15), but so would the people for their wickedness (see verses 16–18; 5:31).

17. VIRGIN DAUGHTER: Judah is so called, having never before been under foreign bondage.

18. A LAND THEY DO NOT KNOW: Babylon.

19–20. UTTERLY REJECTED JUDAH: Lest the Lord be casting Judah off forever, the prophet in deep contrition confesses the nation's sin (see Daniel 9:4ff.).

21. THE THRONE OF YOUR GLORY: Jerusalem, where the temple is located.

15:1–9. EVEN IF MOSES ... SAMUEL: It was ineffective at this point to intercede for the nation. Even prayers by Moses (see Numbers 14:11–25) and Samuel (see 1 Samuel 12:19–25), eminent in intercession, would not defer judgment where unrepentance persists (see Jeremiah 18:8; 26:3). Chief among issues provoking God's judgment was the intense sin of King Manasseh (695–642 BC). Noted in verse 4, this provocation is recounted in 2 Kings 21:1–18, which says the Lord did not relent from His anger because of this (see also 2 Kings 23:26; 24:3–4).

6. I AM WEARY OF RELENTING: God often withholds the judgment He threatens (see Jeremiah 26:19; Exodus 32:14; 1 Chronicles 21:15), sparing people so His patience might lead them to repentance (see Romans 2:4–5; 3:25).

9. SUN ... GONE DOWN WHILE ... YET DAY: Young mothers die in youth and their children are killed.

10. WOE IS ME: Overcome by grief (see Jeremiah 9:1), the prophet wished that he had not been born (see 20:14–18). He had not been a bad or disagreeable creditor or debtor, yet his people cursed him, and he felt the sting.

11–14. YOUR REMNANT: In the midst of judgment, the Lord promised protection for the obedient remnant in Judah (see Malachi 3:16–17). The Babylonians permitted some people to stay in the land when they departed (see Jeremiah 40:5–7). Jeremiah personally received kind treatment from the invader (see 40:1–6); his enemies in Judah would later appeal to him (see 21:1–6; 37:3; 42:1–6). Ultimately, a band of renegade Judeans took Jeremiah to Egypt, against God's will (see 43:1–7).

15–18. O LORD, YOU KNOW: Jeremiah, in a mood of self-pity, reminded the Lord of his faithfulness in bearing reproach, his love for His Word, and his separation from evil people to stand alone.

18. AN UNRELIABLE STREAM: Jeremiah asked that the Lord not fail him like a wadi that has dried up. The answer to this concern is in 2:13 (the Lord is his fountain). See 15:19–21; 17:5–8.

19. IF YOU RETURN, THEN I WILL BRING YOU BACK: The Lord reprimanded the prophet for self-pity and impatience. He had to have the proper posture before God and repent. If he did so, he would be discerning ("take out the precious," a figure drawn from removing pure metal from dross) and have the further privilege of being God's mouthpiece. God urged him to let sinners change to his values but never to compromise. As a man who was to assay and test others (see 6:27–30), he must first assay himself (see the example of Moses in Exodus 4:22–26).

20–21. I WILL DELIVER YOU: When Jeremiah repents, God will protect him (see verses 20–21; see also 1:18–19).

JEREMIAH'S LIFESTYLE AND MESSAGE: As Jeremiah continues his fifth message against Judah (14:1–17:18), the Lord instructs him not to have a wife and family.

16:4. THEY SHALL DIE: Since destruction and exile are soon to fall on Judah, the prophet must not have a wife and family. God's kindness will keep him from anxiety over them in the awful situation of suffering and death (see verse 4; see also 15:9; 1 Corinthians 7:26).

5. THE HOUSE OF MOURNING: This was a home where friends prepared a meal for a bereaved family. Jeremiah is told not to mourn with them or rejoice (see verse 8).

6. CUT . . . BALD: These acts indicated extreme grief.

10–13. Why has the Lord pronounced all this great disaster against us: Jeremiah was to explain the reason for the judgment; that is, the people's forsaking God and worshiping false gods (see verse 11; 2:13). They would get their fill of idols in Babylon (see verse 13).

14–15. no more be said: In view of the Lord's promise of restoration from Babylon, the proof of God's redemptive power and faithfulness in delivering Israel from Egypt would give way to a greater demonstration in the deliverance of His people from Babylon. This bondage was to be so severe that deliverance from Babylon would be a greater relief than from Egypt.

15. all the lands: This reference is extensive enough to be fully realized only in the final gathering into Messiah's earthly kingdom.

16. many fishermen ... hunters: These are references to Babylonian soldiers, who were doing God's judgment work (see verse 17).

18. repay double: The word for "double" signified "full" or "complete," a fitting punishment for such severe sins.

19–21. shall come to You: The result of God's judgment on the Jews will be the end of idolatry; even some Gentiles, witnessing the severity, will renounce idols. After the return from Babylon, this was partly fulfilled as the Jews entirely and permanently renounced idols, and many Gentiles turned from their idols to Jehovah. However, the complete fulfillment will come in the final restoration of Israel (see Isaiah 2:1–4; 49:6; 60:3).

17:1. The sin of Judah: Reasons for the judgment (mentioned in chapter 16) continue here: (1) idolatry (verses 1–4), (2) relying on the flesh (verse 5), and (3) dishonesty in amassing wealth (verse 11).

pen of iron: The names of idols were engraved on the horns of their altars with such a tool. The idea is that Judah's sin was permanent, etched in them as if in stone. It was very different to have God's word written on the heart (see Jeremiah 31:33).

3. My mountain in the field: Jerusalem in Judah.

4. land ... you do not know: Babylon.

5–8. Cursed is the man: Jeremiah contrasted the person who experiences barrenness (see verses 5–6) with the one who receives blessing (see verses 7–8). The difference in attitude involves "trust" placed in man or "trust" vested in the Lord (see verses 5, 7). And the contrast in vitality is between being like a parched dwarf juniper in the desert (see verse 6) or a tree drawing sustenance from a stream to bear fruit (see verse 8; see also Psalm 1:1–3).

10. I . . . SEARCH THE HEART: For the sin of man (verses 1–4), for the barren man (verses 5, 6), or the blessed man (verses 7–8), God is the final Judge and renders His judgment for their works (see Revelation 20:11–15). By Him, actions are weighed (see 1 Samuel 2:3).

11. A PARTRIDGE: This referred to a sand grouse that invaded and brooded over a nest not its own but was forced to leave before the eggs hatched. It depicted a person who unjustly took possession of things he had no right to take but couldn't enjoy the benefits, despite all the effort.

14–18. SAVE ME, AND I SHALL BE SAVED: Jeremiah voiced the prayerful cry that God would deliver him from his enemies (see verse 14). Surrounded by ungodly people (see verses 1–6, 11, 13), he showed qualities of godliness: (1) God was his praise (see verse 14); (2) he had a shepherd's heart to follow God (see verse 16); (3) he was a man of prayer, open to God's examination (see verse 16); (4) God was his hope (see verse 17); and (5) he trusted God's faithfulness to deliver, even in judgment (see verse 18).

UNLEASHING THE TEXT

1) Jeremiah asked the Lord, "Why does the way of the wicked prosper?" (12:1). What is the biblical answer to this question?

_____

_____

_____

_____

_____

2) In chapter 13, Jeremiah highlighted a linen sash and wine bottles that were used as part of his teaching. What was God communicating through those symbols?

_____

_____

_____

_____

_____

_____

3) What do you learn about God's nature and character from Jeremiah 15:1–9?

_____

_____

_____

_____

_____

_____

_____

_____

4) Look again at Jeremiah 17:19–27, which concerns God's regulations in regard to the Sabbath. What did God expect from His people on that day?

_____

_____

_____

_____

_____

_____

_____

_____

EXPLORING THE MEANING

The people had earned God's judgment. When Jeremiah looked at the situation in Judah, he asked the Lord, "Why does the way of the wicked prosper? Why are those happy who deal so treacherously?" (12:1). The prophet even had a suggestion for how God should deal with those who preyed on their fellow Israelites: "Pull them out like sheep for the slaughter, and prepare them for the day of slaughter" (verse 3). God, in answering His prophet, confirmed that the people of Judah would receive the consequences of their collective sin. In particular, God spoke about "plunderers" who would appear on the horizon to punish His people. This invasion would not be a random attack but rather was God's appointed judgment—"the sword of the Lord" that would "devour from one end of the land to the other end of the land" (verse 12). At the end of God's answer to Jeremiah, He used language connected to the seasonal harvest: "They have sown wheat but reaped thorns. . . . But be ashamed of your harvest because of the fierce anger of the LORD" (verse 13). As a nation, Judah had earned her judgment through generations of injustice, idolatry, and rebellion against God.

The people were puffed up by pride. As mentioned in the previous lesson, God was still willing to withhold His judgment from Judah even at such a late hour. He had sent Jeremiah to confront the people with their unrighteousness and call them back to Himself through repentance. "Say to the king and to the queen mother, 'Humble yourselves; sit down, for your rule shall collapse, the crown of your glory.' The cities of the South shall be shut up, and no one shall open them; Judah shall be carried away captive, all of it; it shall be wholly carried away captive" (13:18–19). Sadly, the people did not listen. Why? One reason was pride. Jeremiah cried out to the people, "Hear and give ear: Do not be proud, for the LORD has spoken" (verse 15). But still, they refused to repent. Even God mourned the pride of His people: "But if you will not hear it, My soul will weep in secret for your pride . . . because the LORD's flock has been taken captive" (verse 17). Today, pride is still one of the core obstacles that hinders people from responding to the gospel. People who overly esteem themselves to be wise, strong, or righteous will often refuse to believe the necessity of receiving forgiveness for their sin.

The people ignored important warnings. Jeremiah 14 begins the prophet's fifth message to the people of Judah. Importantly, the prophet delivered the message during a time of drought. In fact, this "word of the LORD" was specifically "concerning the droughts" (verse 1). The presence of droughts in the land should have been a warning sign to the people living there. Long ago in God's covenant with Moses, the Lord described the conditions that would produce blessings or curses in the promised land: "If you walk in My statutes and keep My commandments, and perform them, then I will give you rain in its season, the land shall yield its produce, and the trees of the field shall yield their fruit" (Leviticus 26:3–4). On the other hand: "If you do not obey Me, and do not observe all these commandments . . . I will make your heavens like iron and your earth like bronze. And your strength shall be spent in vain; for your land shall not yield its produce, nor shall the trees of the land yield their fruit" (verses 14, 19–20). A prolonged drought in Judah should have awoken its leaders to the reality of their sin. The lack of water and fruitfulness was a direct warning from God—a sign that they again ignored.

REFLECTING ON THE TEXT

5) People often respond to negative circumstances by labeling them "unfair." How would you describe our culture's opinions when it comes to the reason for suffering in this world?

_____

_____

_____

_____

_____

6) Do you think that God still judges, rewards, and punishes groups of people at the level of nations? Explain your response.

_____

_____

_____

_____

_____

7) What are some ways that our culture attempts to produce or inflate pride within people?

_____

_____

_____

_____

8) What are some methods God uses to warn people today about the coming consequences of their actions and sinful choices?

_____

_____

_____

_____

_____

PERSONAL RESPONSE

9) Where do you see evidence of unhealthy pride in your life? What are some possible consequences of that pride?

_____

_____

_____

_____

_____

_____

10) What steps will you take this week to seek out the conviction and direction of the Holy Spirit? (In other words, how will you actively start to look for His warnings now rather than wait for the future consequences of poor decisions?)

_____

_____

_____

_____

_____

4

IN THE POTTER'S HOUSE
Jeremiah 17:19–20:18

DRAWING NEAR

What are some good qualities that you possess? Do those qualities characterize your life? Explain your response.

_____

_____

_____

_____

_____

_____

_____

_____

_____

_____

_____

_____

_____

_____

_____

_____

_____

_____

THE CONTEXT

The book of Jeremiah is a mix of prophetic messages interspersed with biographical details about the prophet's life—specifically, his interactions with God and those in Judah he was called to confront. These biographical interludes do not all occur in chronological order. Some events are included outside a sequential timeline in order to emphasize important themes. For example, several of Jeremiah's prophecies occurred during the fourth year of King Jehoiakim's reign in Judah, yet those prophecies are spread throughout Jeremiah's prophetic record. One such message begins in chapter 25, another in chapter 36, and another in chapter 45.

In this lesson, we will explore two more of Jeremiah's messages to the people of Judah in chapters 17–20. Jeremiah's sixth message (17:21–24) deals with the people's failure to observe the Sabbath. His seventh message (18:1–20:18) centers on two object lessons. The first involves the prophet's observations at a potter's house and includes God's famous declaration, "O house of Israel, can I not do with you as this potter? . . . Look, as the clay is in the potter's hand, so are you in My hand, O house of Israel!" (18:6). The second object lesson includes a confrontation with priests and elders in the Valley of Hinnom—a place known for child sacrifice.

In chapter 20, Jeremiah describes a notable confrontation he had with a man named Pashhur, who was a priest and "chief governor in the house of the LORD" (verse 1). Pashhur, having heard Jeremiah's claim that God would allow Babylon to overwhelm Jerusalem and tear down the temple, physically struck the prophet and placed him in stocks. He did this both to punish Jeremiah and publicly humiliate him—an offense for which he later paid dearly.

KEYS TO THE TEXT

Read Jeremiah 17:19–20:18, noting the key words and phrases indicated below.

> JEREMIAH'S SIXTH MESSAGE: *In Jeremiah's brief sixth message (17:19–27), he addresses the sin of the people in not keeping the Sabbath.*

17:21–24. SABBATH DAY: Not only had the Jews failed to observe Sabbath days, but the required Sabbath year of rest for the land (Leviticus 25:1–7) was regularly violated as well. God had warned that such disobedience would bring judgment (see Leviticus 26:34–35, 43; 2 Chronicles 36:20, 21). The seventy-year captivity was correlated to the 490 years from Saul to the captivity, which included seventy Sabbath years. When the Jews were restored from captivity, special emphasis was placed on Sabbath faithfulness (see Nehemiah 13:19).

25–27. THRONE OF DAVID: For their obedience, God would assure the dynasty of David perpetual rule in Jerusalem, safety for the city, and worship at the temple. But continued disobedience would meet with destruction of the city. (See note on Jeremiah 22:2, 4.)

> *JEREMIAH'S SEVENTH MESSAGE: A close link exists between chapter 17 and Jeremiah's seventh message against Judah in chapters 18–20. Destruction is in view in chapter 17, but repentance can yet prevent it (see 18:7–8). However, repentance was not forthcoming, so Jeremiah's shattered earthen flask illustrated God's violent judgment on Israel (chapter 19). Then, their rejection of God's Word (see 19:15) led to persecution against God's mouthpiece in chapter 20.*

18:2–6. POTTER'S HOUSE: God sent Jeremiah to a potter, who gave him an illustration by shaping a vessel. The prophet secured a vessel and used it for his own illustration (see 19:1ff.). Jeremiah watched the potter at his wheel. The soft clay became misshapen, but the potter shaped it back into a good vessel. God would so do with Judah, if she repented.

8–10. TURNS FROM ITS EVIL: Although the Lord had announced impending judgment, the "marred" nation could be restored as a good vessel by God, who would hold off the judgment (see verses 8, 11). By contrast, if the nation continued in sin, He would not bring the blessing desired (see verses 9–10).

12. THAT IS HOPELESS: Jeremiah brought the people to the point where they actually stated their condition honestly. The prophet's threats were useless because they were so far gone—abandoned to their sins and the penalty. All hypocrisy was abandoned in favor of honesty, but repentance was not in Israel (as in verse 18; 19:15). This explains a seeming paradox, that Israel could repent and avert judgment, yet Jeremiah was not to pray for Israel (see 7:16; 11:14). It would do no good to pray for their change, as they had steeled themselves against any spiritual change.

13. VIRGIN OF ISRAEL: That Israel was the virgin whom God had chosen (see 2 Kings 19:21) only enhanced their guilt.

14. SNOW WATER . . . COLD FLOWING WATERS: No reasonable person would forsake such for "the rock of the field," perhaps a poetic term for Mount Lebanon, from which the high mountain streams flowed. Yet Israel forsook God, the fountain of living waters, for broken foreign cisterns (see Jeremiah 2:13).

18. PLANS AGAINST JEREMIAH: Plans to indict the prophet with their "tongues" and then to kill him (see verse 23) were based on the premise that his message of doom was not true. The business of the priests, the wise, and the prophets continued as usual, because God made them lasting institutions (see Leviticus 6:18; 10:11).

19–23. GIVE HEED TO ME: This is one of many examples of human prayer aligning with God's will as Jeremiah prays for God's work of judgment to be done (see verses 11, 15–17).

22. DUG A PIT: See Jeremiah 38:6.

THE SIGN OF THE BROKEN FLASK: Jeremiah continues his seventh message (18:1–20:18) with an object lesson for the elders of the people and the priests.

19:1. ELDERS OF THE PEOPLE . . . THE PRIESTS: These were chosen to be credible witnesses of the symbolic action with the "earthen flask" so no one could plead ignorance of the prophecy. The seventy-two elders who made up the Sanhedrin were partly from the "priests" and the other tribes ("people").

2. VALLEY . . . HINNOM: See note on 19:6.

POTSHERD GATE: The gate of "broken pottery" was on the south wall of Jerusalem where the potters formed pottery for use in the temple nearby.

6. TOPHET: Hebrew uses the word *toph* for "drum." This was another name for the Valley of Hinnom, an east-west valley at the south end of Jerusalem where, when children were burned as sacrifices to idols (see verses 4–5), drums were beaten to drown out their cries. Rubbish from Jerusalem was dumped there and continually burned (see 2 Kings 23:10). The place became a symbol for the burning fires of hell, called Gehenna (see Matthew 5:22). See Jeremiah 7:30–32; Isaiah 30:33. It was to become a place of massacre.

9. EAT THE FLESH: Desperate for food during a long siege, some would resort to cannibalism, eating family members and friends (see Lamentations 4:10).

10. THE MEN WHO GO WITH YOU: See Jeremiah 19:1.

13. DEFILED: Their houses were desecrated by idolatrous worship.

INCENSE TO...HOST OF HEAVEN: This refers to worship of the sun, planets, and stars from flat housetops (see Jeremiah 32:29; 2 Kings 23:11–12; Zephaniah 1:5).

JEREMIAH'S UNPOPULAR MINISTRY: Jeremiah interrupts his seventh message (18:1–20:18) with an account of his mistreatment at the hands of a priest named Pashhur.

20:1. PASHHUR: The meaning of the name is either "ease" or "deliverance is round about," both in contrast to the new name that God will assign him in verse 3. He was one of several men so named (see Jeremiah 21:1; 38:1).

IMMER: He was one of the original "governors of the sanctuary" (see 1 Chronicles 24:14).

CHIEF GOVERNOR: He was not the high priest but the chief official in charge of temple police, who were to maintain order.

2. STRUCK JEREMIAH: Pashhur, or others acting on his authority, delivered forty lashes (see Deuteronomy 25:3) to the prophet.

PUT HIM IN THE STOCKS: Hands, feet, and neck were fastened in holes, bending the body to a distorted posture, causing excruciating pain.

HIGH GATE: The northern gate of the upper temple court.

3. MAGOR-MISSABIB: "Terror on every side" is the fitting name God reckons for the leader. The details of that terror are outlined in verses 4 and 6 (see also 6:25).

4. BABYLON: This was Jeremiah's direct identification of the conqueror who would come out of the "north" (1:13), from "a far country" (4:16).

8. DERISION DAILY: In verses 7–18, Jeremiah prayerfully lamented the ridicule he was experiencing because of God's role for his life. His feelings wavered between quitting (see verse 9a), being encouraged (see verses 9c, 11), petitioning for help (see verse 12), praise (see verse 13), and waves of depression (see verses 14–18; see also 11:18–23; 15:10, 15–18).

9. I WILL NOT MAKE MENTION: A surge of dejection swept over Jeremiah, making him long to say no more. But being compelled within (see Job 32:18–19; Psalm 39:3; Acts 18:5; 1 Corinthians 9:16–17) because he did not want his enemies to see him fail (see verse 10), he experienced the presence of the Lord (see verse 11) and remembered God's previous deliverances (see verse 13).

14. CURSED BE THE DAY: Another tide of depression engulfed the prophet, perhaps when he was in the painful stocks (see verse 2). His words are like Job's (see Job 3:3, 10–11).

15. LET THE MAN BE CURSED: The servant of God fell into sinful despair and questioned the wisdom and purpose of God, for which he should have been thankful.

16. THE CITIES WHICH THE LORD OVERTHREW: Sodom and Gomorrah (see Genesis 19:25).

UNLEASHING THE TEXT

1) Where do you see evidence in these chapters of Jeremiah that you explored in this lesson that the people of Judah could have avoided God's judgment?

_____

_____

_____

_____

_____

_____

2) What lesson was God teaching Jeremiah at the potter's house (see 18:1–11)?

_____

_____

_____

_____

_____

_____

3) How would you summarize God's message to the people of Judah in chapter 19? What was the purpose of the broken flask (see verse 10)?

_____

_____

_____

_____

_____

_____

4) Jeremiah describes some of the persecution that he endured as a prophet of the Lord in 18:18–23 and 20:1–18. What do you learn about Jeremiah from those passages?

_____

_____

_____

_____

_____

_____

_____

_____

EXPLORING THE MEANING

The potter's house revealed God's sovereignty. Jeremiah 18 includes a famous illustration in which the prophet watched a potter at work. As the potter worked his wheel to make a clay vessel of some kind, it became "marred" (verse 4) and corrupted in some way. However, because the clay was soft and pliable, the potter was able to reshape it into something new—and something useful. As Jeremiah watched that scene, the word of the Lord came to him: "'O house of Israel, can I not do with you as this potter?' says the LORD. 'Look, as the clay is in the potter's hand, so are you in My hand, O house of Israel!'" (verse 6). This is a picture of God's sovereignty. No matter how much we cling to our desires to control our world and our future, the reality is that God alone is sovereign over all things. The prophet Isaiah expressed a similar sentiment: "O LORD, You are our Father; we are the clay, and You our potter; and all we are the work of Your hand" (64:8). As did Paul: "Does not the potter have power over the clay, from the same lump to make one vessel for honor and another for dishonor?" (Romans 9:21).

The potter's house revealed Judah's opportunity. The "marring" of the clay vessel in the potter's house was an important image for the Jewish people of Jeremiah's day. They were God's chosen people, and He had planned to reveal Himself to the whole world through this special relationship and through His covenants with Israel. Yet over the course of generations, the people had rejected the Lord and turned aside from those covenants. They had become "marred." Even so, God made it clear the opportunity still existed for them to repent and avoid His wrath: "The instant I speak concerning a nation and concerning a kingdom, to pluck up, to pull down, and to destroy it, if that nation against whom I have spoken turns from its evil, I will relent of the disaster that I thought to bring upon it" (18:7–8). God then added, "Behold, I am fashioning a disaster and devising a plan against you. Return now every one from his evil way, and make your ways and your doings good" (verse 11). But once again, the people refused to seize the opportunity. They told Jeremiah, "That is hopeless! So we will walk according to our own plans, and we will every one obey the dictates of his evil heart" (verse 12).

The potter's flask revealed Judah's future. Because the people of Judah chose to obey their evil hearts rather than return to the Lord, their future became sealed. Babylon would invade from the north, bringing destruction, ruin, hunger, and captivity on a scale the people had never seen. Jeremiah illustrated this future reality with another object lesson—this time, a potter's flask. God commanded Jeremiah to gather several elders and priests and take them outside the Potsherd Gate of Jerusalem. This gate led to a place known as the Valley of Hinnom (or Tophet), a refuse dump for Jerusalem where trash was burned regularly and the fires rarely went out. It was a place of dust, a place of broken shards of pottery, and—most vile—a place where children were offered in the flames as a sacrifice to Molech. In that evil place, Jeremiah smashed the potter's flask to symbolize what would happen to Jerusalem. What used to be called the Valley of Hinnom would become the Valley of Slaughter. "Thus says the LORD of hosts: 'Even so I will break this people and this city, as one breaks a potter's vessel, which cannot be made whole again; and they shall bury them in Tophet till there is no place to bury" (19:11).

REFLECTING ON THE TEXT

5) What does God's sovereignty mean for your life? How does His sovereignty harmonize with free will?

---

6) What are some possible explanations as to why the people of Judah chose to walk "according to [their] own plans" (Jeremiah 18:12) rather than return to the Lord?

_____

_____

_____

_____

_____

7) What are some symptoms in people's lives that reveal they are relying on themselves rather than listening to God?

_____

_____

_____

_____

_____

8) Which of the evils in our culture feels the most evident to you right now? What are some ways the church can work to confront those evils?

_____

_____

_____

_____

_____

PERSONAL RESPONSE

9) In what areas of life are you currently resisting God's sovereignty? Where are you seeking to have your own way?

_____

_____

_____

_____

_____

10) Where do you currently have an opportunity to stand against evil or corruption in your community?

_____

_____

_____

_____

_____

_____

_____

_____

5

GOD REJECTS THE KING'S REQUEST
Jeremiah 21:1–24:10

DRAWING NEAR
What are some major prayer requests that God has answered or provided for in your life?

_____

_____

_____

_____

_____

_____

_____

_____

_____

_____

_____

_____

_____

_____

_____

_____

THE CONTEXT
For much of Jeremiah's prophetic record up to this point, the threat of Babylon loomed on the horizon. God, through His prophet, reminded His people again

and again that they would experience siege and suffering at the hands of a threat from the north. Over time, as Jeremiah's prophecies became more specific, King Nebuchadnezzar and his armies were identified as the instrument God would use to humble His people. Geographically, the ancient city of Babylon was located in modern-day Iraq, likely about fifty miles south of Baghdad on the Euphrates River. The distance between Babylon and Jerusalem was more than 700 miles.

Critically, the Babylonians did not overwhelm Judah and Jerusalem in a single attack. Starting around 607 BC, Nebuchadnezzar came against Judah and forced its king to become his vassal—meaning that the leaders of Judah paid tribute (taxes) to Babylon. It was during this time that Daniel and his companions, along with many others from among the best and brightest of the Jews, were taken to Babylon as captives. Three years later, King Jehoiakim attempted to throw off the Babylonian yolk, turning to Egypt in an effort to break free. But the effort failed, resulting in a siege around Jerusalem. After massive suffering, Jerusalem again submitted to Nebuchadnezzar in 597 BC. Zedekiah was named the new king of Judah.

Nine years later, Zedekiah attempted to join forces with other vassal nations in another revolt against Nebuchadnezzar. Once again, the attempt failed. This time, in 588 BC, the armies of Babylon surrounded Jerusalem in a siege that lasted for thirty months. They overwhelmed the city, broke down its walls, and destroyed its temple—all as Jeremiah had prophesied.

KEYS TO THE TEXT

Read Jeremiah 21:1–24:10, noting the key words and phrases indicated below.

> *JEREMIAH'S EIGHTH MESSAGE: Jeremiah delivers his eighth message against Judah (21:1–14) during the final siege by King Nebuchadnezzar of Babylon, resulting in the third and final deportation of the Jewish people from their homeland.*

21:1. KING ZEDEKIAH. See 2 Kings 24:17–25:7 for the details of his reign (c. 597–586 BC).

PASHHUR: This was a different priest than the man by this name in Jeremiah 20:1–6.

2. WAR AGAINST US: King Zedekiah hoped for God's intervention, such as Hezekiah had received against Sennacherib (see 2 Kings 19:35–36).

4. TURN BACK THE WEAPONS . . . ASSEMBLE THEM: The Jews were already fighting the invaders by going outside the walls of the city to battle them on the hillsides and in the valleys as they approached. However, they would soon be driven back into the city, where the enemy would collect all their weapons and execute many with those very weapons.

5. I MYSELF WILL FIGHT: God used an invader as His instrument of judgment (see verse 7). The Jews have not only the Babylonians as their enemy but also God.

7. STRIKE THEM . . . SWORD: This was the fate of Zedekiah's son and many nobles. Zedekiah died of grief (see Jeremiah 34:4; 2 Kings 25:6–8).

8–9. LIFE AND . . . DEATH: Since a persistent lack of repentance had led to the conquest, Jeremiah urged the Jews to submit and surrender to the besieger so they would be treated as captives of war and live, rather than be killed.

12. O HOUSE OF DAVID: The royal family and all connected with it were called on to enact justice and righteousness promptly ("morning"). There was still time for them to escape the destruction, if there was repentance.

13. INHABITANT OF THE VALLEY . . . ROCK OF THE PLAIN: Jerusalem is personified as dwelling among rocks, hills, and valleys.

14. I WILL PUNISH: During the siege, Jerusalem will be burned (see verse 10), as will the land in general.

> JEREMIAH'S NINTH MESSAGE: *Jeremiah addresses the people of Judah with a ninth message of judgment (22:1–23:40) that includes a reference to the throne of David—a reminder of the Davidic covenant of 2 Samuel 7:3–17, in which God promised David that his heirs would rule over Israel.*

22:6. GILEAD . . . LEBANON: The beautiful high mountains of the land.

7. CUT DOWN . . . CHOICE CEDARS: This could refer primarily to the palaces and great houses built from such timber (see Song of Solomon 1:17).

10. THE DEAD: This is probably a reference to Josiah, who died before the destruction (see 2 Kings 22:20; Isaiah 57:1). Dying saints are to be envied; living sinners pitied. When Josiah died, and on each anniversary of his death, there was public weeping in which Jeremiah participated (see 2 Chronicles 35:24–25).

11–12. SHALLUM: This is another name for King Jehoahaz, who reigned for three months (609 BC; see 2 Kings 23:31). He was the fourth son of Josiah (see

1 Chronicles 3:15). The name was given to him in irony, because the people called him Shalom ("peace"), but Shallum means "retribution."

13–17. WOE TO HIM: This message indicted Jehoahaz (see verses 13–14, 17), who was unlike his father, the good king, Josiah (verses 15–16).

18–19. JEHOIAKIM: Ruling from 609 to 598 BC, he wickedly taxed the people (see 2 Kings 23:35) and made them build his palace without pay, violating God's law in Leviticus 19:13 and Deuteronomy 24:14–15 (see also Micah 3:10; Habakkuk 2:9; James 5:4). He was killed in Babylon's second siege. His corpse was dishonored and left like a dead donkey on the ground for scavengers to feed on.

20. GO UP TO LEBANON: Sinners dwelling in the northwest in Lebanon's cedar land and others to the northeast beyond the Sea of Galilee in Bashan would suffer in the invasion. The entire land would come under judgment as Abarim in the southeast.

24–26. CONIAH: A short form of Jeconiah, perhaps used in contempt, who was also called Jehoiachin. He ruled only three months and ten days (see 2 Chronicles 36:9) in 598–597 BC, and then was taken into captivity, where he lived out his life.

24. SIGNET: A ring with a personal insignia on it (see Haggai 2:23).

28. IS THIS . . . WHY ARE THEY: Questions the people who idolized Jeconiah were asking.

30. WRITE . . . AS CHILDLESS: Jeconiah did have offspring (see 1 Chronicles 3:17–18), but he was reckoned childless in the sense that he had no sons who would reign ("sitting on the throne"). The curse continued in his descendants down to Joseph, the husband of Mary. How could Jesus then be the Messiah when His father was under this curse? It was because Joseph was not involved in the bloodline of Jesus, since He was virgin born (see Matthew 1:12). Jesus' blood right to the throne of David came through Mary from Nathan, Solomon's brother, not Solomon (Jeconiah's line), thus bypassing this curse (see Luke 3:31–32). See Jeremiah 36:30.

23:1–2. WOE TO THE SHEPHERDS: See note on Jeremiah 6:3. These "shepherds" were false leaders who failed in their duty to assure the people's welfare (see verse 2), starting with the kings in chapter 22 and other civil heads, as well as prophets and priests (see verse 11). They stood in contrast to the shepherds whom God would later give the nation (see verse 4; 3:15). Other significant chapters in the Bible that condemn evil shepherds and false prophets include Jeremiah 14; 27; 28; Isaiah 28; Ezekiel 13; 34; Micah 3; and Zechariah 11.

3–4. I WILL GATHER: God pledged to restore exiled Israelites to their ancient soil. Similar promises are given in Jeremiah 16:14–15 and chapters 30–33. The land in view was literally Palestine, being contrasted with the other countries (see verse 3), thus assuring that the regathering would be as literal as the scattering. The restoration of Judah from Babylon is referred to in language that, in its fullness, can only refer to the final restoration of God's people ("out of all countries," verse 8), under the Messiah. "Neither shall they be lacking" indicates no one will be missing or detached. See Jeremiah 32:37–38; Isaiah 60:21; Ezekiel 34:11–16.

4. SHEPHERDS . . . WILL FEED THEM: See Ezekiel 34:23–31. Zerubbabel, Ezra, Nehemiah, and others were small fulfillments compared to the consummate shepherding of the Messiah Jesus.

5. BRANCH: The Messiah is pictured as a branch (literally "shoot") out of David's family tree (see Jeremiah 33:15–16; Isaiah 4:2; 11:1–5; Zechariah 3:8; 6:12–13), who will rule over God's people in the future. (See Jeremiah 33:14–17, where the same promise is repeated, and note on 22:2, 4.)

6. THE LORD OUR RIGHTEOUSNESS: This emphasis is stated three times in verses 5 and 6. The Messiah's shepherding is contrasted with that of the false shepherds (see verses 1–2, 11, 14). Judah and Israel will be reunited (see Ezekiel 37:15–23).

7–8. THEY SHALL NO LONGER SAY: See note on Jeremiah 16:14–15.

13–14. SAMARIA . . . ISRAEL: Jerusalem and Judah were worse than Samaria and Israel.

14. A HORRIBLE THING IN THE PROPHETS: The false shepherds told lies, committed adultery, and declared vain dreams (see verses 25, 27). They became like chaff rather than grain (see verse 28), while promising peace (see verse 17) to those whose sins provoke God to bring calamity, not comfort. The scene was like Sodom and Gomorrah, whose sin so grieved God that He destroyed them by fire (see Genesis 19:13, 24–25).

18. WHO HAS STOOD IN THE COUNSEL OF THE LORD: Here was the compelling reason not to listen to the false prophets (see verse 16)—they didn't speak God's Word.

20. LATTER DAYS: They wouldn't listen, but the day would come (see verse 12) when the judgment would fall, and then they would "understand."

21–22. I HAVE NOT SENT THESE PROPHETS: According to the Mosaic Law, these false prophets should have been put to death through stoning (see Deuteronomy 13:1–5; 18:20–22).

23–24. GOD NEAR . . . GOD AFAR OFF: The false prophets were not to think they could hide their devices from God, who declares Himself omnipresent and omniscient, in both an immanent and transcendent sense.

25. I HAVE DREAMED: Here was a claim to divine revelation through dreams (see Numbers 12:6). But such claims were a deception (see verses 26–27), unequal in power to God's Word (see verses 28–29).

29. LIKE A FIRE . . . HAMMER: God's Word has irresistible qualities to prevail over the deception in the shepherds' false messages.

33. THE ORACLE OF THE LORD . . . WHAT ORACLE: The people asked, in mockery, for Jeremiah to give them his latest prophecy ("oracle"). This ridicule of Jeremiah's faithful preaching demanded a response, so God told the prophet to repeat the question and reply simply, "I will even forsake you," meaning judgment from God was certainly coming.

34–40. THE ORACLE OF THE LORD: When a person falsely claimed to have a word from God, he would be punished for perverting God's truth. Claiming to have prophecies from God, when not true, is dangerous to one's well-being.

JEREMIAH'S TENTH MESSAGE: Jeremiah begins his tenth message against Judah (24:1–10) with an object lesson involving two baskets of figs, representing that deported Judeans, captive in Babylon, will have good treatment and not death.

24:1. AFTER NEBUCHADNEZZAR . . . CARRIED AWAY: This refers to Babylon's second deportation of Judeans in 597 BC (see 2 Kings 24:10–17).

5. LIKE THESE GOOD FIGS: The object lesson of verse 2 is here explained. The deported Judeans will be granted privileges as colonists, rather than being enslaved as captives.

6–7. BACK TO THIS LAND: While it is true that a remnant returned to Judah in 538 BC, this promise had greater overtones in regard to the ultimate fulfillment of the Abrahamic (see Genesis 12), Davidic (see 2 Samuel 7), and New Covenants (see Jeremiah 31) in the day of Messiah's coming and kingdom (see Jeremiah 32:41; 33:7). Their conversion (verse 7) from idolatry to the one true God is expressed in language that, in its fullness, applies to their complete conversion in the final kingdom after the present dispersion (see Romans 11:1–5, 25–27).

8–10. AS THE BAD FIGS: Those people remaining at Jerusalem during the eleven years (597–586 BC) of Zedekiah's vassal reign would soon face hardship from further scattering to other countries, violent death, famine, and disease; see Jeremiah 29:17. (See also 25:9 and note there.) These verses quote the curses of Deuteronomy 28:25, 37 (see Jeremiah 29:18, 22; Psalm 44:13, 14) and are also fulfilled in the history of the long dispersion until Messiah returns.

UNLEASHING THE TEXT

1) What was the situation in Judah as the events of Jeremiah 21 began to unfold? What request did King Zedekiah make of the Lord (see verses 1–2)?

_____

_____

_____

_____

_____

2) What do you learn about God from His response to Zedekiah in verses 3–10?

_____

_____

_____

_____

3) What are some specific foreshadowings of Jesus in Jeremiah 23:1–8?

_____

_____

_____

_____

4) The rest of chapter 23 focuses on the false prophets who spoke against Jeremiah in Jerusalem. In what ways did those false prophets lead the people astray?

_____

_____

_____

_____

Exploring the Meaning

The future would bring destruction. For decades, Jeremiah had declared that Jerusalem would be overthrown by invaders from the north. For decades, the people had rebuked Jeremiah and refused to listen to his words. Even after the first two waves of Babylonian attack, in which Nebuchadnezzar took captives and laid siege to Jerusalem, the people believed God would never allow His holy city nor His holy temple to be destroyed. They were wrong. In time, Nebuchadnezzar brought his armies for a third and final attack against Jerusalem. Finally, King Zedekiah understood the reality of his peril and asked Jeremiah to pray that the nation would be spared. Perhaps the king was thinking of the way God had spared Judah during the reign of Hezekiah, when Sennacherib's armies from Assyria were miraculously destroyed (see 2 Kings 19:35–36). But God responded by unambiguously rejecting Zedekiah's request: "I Myself will fight against you with an outstretched hand and with a strong arm, even in anger and fury and great wrath" (Jeremiah 21:5). There would be no miracle ending and no salvation in the short term. The opportunity for repentance had come and gone, and judgment was now at hand.

The future would bring captivity. God did extend one word of advice to His people: "Behold, I set before you the way of life and the way of death. He who remains in this city shall die by the sword, by famine, and by pestilence; but he who goes out and defects to the Chaldeans who besiege you, he shall live, and his life shall be as a prize to him. For I have set My face against this city for adversity and not for good. . . . It shall be given into the hand of the king of Babylon, and he shall burn it with fire" (Jeremiah 21:8–10). A siege was a terrible event in the ancient world—a strategy both brutal and effective. When an attacking army surrounded a city, soldiers cut off all supplies and sources of aid, often for months and years. Those inside the city dealt with starvation, poor hygiene, loss of work and purpose, and the worst elements of human nature. God recommended the people of Jerusalem spare themselves from that misery by surrendering to Babylon. God Himself had declared that Babylon would be victorious; therefore, resistance was pointless. The people of Judah *would* be carried off into captivity.

The future would bring salvation. In the short term, Jeremiah declared that Jerusalem would be destroyed and its people taken away as captives into

Babylon. The people's fate was sealed because of their continued rebellion against God and refusal to repent. In the long term, however, God promised a different outcome. Specifically, He promised that a day would come when Jews scattered throughout the ancient world would return and rebuild Jerusalem: "But I will gather the remnant of My flock out of all countries where I have driven them, and bring them back to their folds; and they shall be fruitful and increase" (Jeremiah 23:3). This prophecy was fulfilled within decades when Nehemiah, Ezra, and others returned from Babylon, restored the city walls, and rebuilt the temple. But God offered an even greater promise farther out into the future: salvation. Jeremiah prophesied about a "Branch of righteousness" (verse 5) that would come from David's line. "In His days Judah will be saved, and Israel will dwell safely; now this is His name by which He will be called: THE LORD OUR RIGHTEOUSNESS" (verse 6). This prophecy was fulfilled in the incarnation, ministry, death, and resurrection of Jesus Christ.

REFLECTING ON THE TEXT

5) Why are judgment and wrath essential elements of God's character? Why are they necessary in our world?

_____

_____

_____

_____

_____

_____

_____

6) What did the people of Judah need to give up or surrender in order to accept God's declaration of captivity in Babylon?

_____

_____

_____

_____

_____

_____

_____

7) As a follower of Jesus, what does God call you to give up or surrender as you serve Him in your culture and in your community?

_____

_____

_____

_____

_____

8) Think for a moment on the name "THE LORD OUR RIGHTEOUSNESS" (Jeremiah 23:6). How does that name reflect your relationship with Jesus?

_____

_____

_____

_____

_____

PERSONAL RESPONSE

9) When have you recently experienced God's discipline or correction? How did you respond?

_____

_____

_____

_____

_____

10) What is holding you back from fully submitting to God?

_____

_____

_____

_____

_____

_____

6

Judah's Seventy-Year Captivity
Jeremiah 25:1–29:32

Drawing Near

If you had to choose another country in which to live out the rest of your life, where would you go? Why would you choose that particular place to live?

_____

_____

_____

_____

_____

_____

_____

_____

_____

_____

_____

_____

_____

The Context

As a reminder, the prophetic messages and biographical content recorded by Jeremiah do not follow a linear or chronological pattern. Instead, the content jumps around between time periods. Jeremiah did this in order to emphasize specific themes, contrast the behavior of specific people, highlight similar judgments proclaimed against multiple nations, and so on.

Chapter 25 contains Jeremiah's eleventh message to the people of Judah and Jerusalem, but it jumps back to the first year of Nebuchadnezzar's reign (605 BC). Chapter 26 is more biographical and goes back another four years to 609 BC, which was the first year of King Jehoiakim in Judah. Specifically, that chapter details the way priests and other leaders responded to Jeremiah's early prophecies of judgment, seeking to take his life because he proclaimed doom over the city. Ultimately, Jeremiah's life was spared, as God had promised.

Chapters 27 and 28 record the thirteenth of Jeremiah's prophetic messages, in which he wore a yoke around his neck to symbolize the way that Babylon would make vassals of Judah, Edom, Moab, Tyre, Sidon, and other nations. Jeremiah's fourteenth message is recorded in chapter 29 as a letter to comfort those who had been taken into exile in 597 BC.

At the heart of all these prophecies was the promise that Judah's exile would only last for seventy years: "This whole land shall be a desolation and an astonishment, and these nations shall serve the king of Babylon seventy years" (Jeremiah 25:11). "For thus says the LORD: After seventy years are completed at Babylon, I will visit you and perform My good word toward you, and cause you to return to this place" (29:10). This crucial promise would become a beacon of hope for those taken in exile, including men such as Daniel, Ezra, and Nehemiah.

KEYS TO THE TEXT

Read Jeremiah 25:1–29:32, noting the key words and phrases indicated below.

> JEREMIAH'S ELEVENTH MESSAGE: *Jeremiah delivers his eleventh message against Judah (25:1–38) during the fourth year of Jehoiakim's reign, which would put the date at 605/604 BC, as Jehoiakim reigned from 609–598 BC.*

25:1. THE FIRST YEAR OF NEBUCHADNEZZAR: Nebuchadnezzar reigned from 605–562 BC.

3. THIRTEENTH YEAR OF JOSIAH: The time is c. 627/626 BC. Josiah ruled from 640–609 BC.

TWENTY-THIRD YEAR: Jeremiah began his ministry in the thirteenth year of Josiah (see 1:2) and had been faithful to preach repentance and judgment for twenty-three years (c. 605/604 BC).

9. MY SERVANT: God used a pagan king, Nebuchadnezzar, to accomplish His will (see also Isaiah 45:1, where God used Cyrus of Persia in a similar manner).

10. VOICE OF MIRTH: See Jeremiah 7:34; see also Revelation 18:23.

11. SEVENTY YEARS: Here is the first specific statement on the length of the Exile (see Jeremiah 29:10). This period probably began in the fourth year of Jehoiakim, when Jerusalem was first captured and the temple treasures were taken. It ended with the decree of Cyrus that allowed the Jews to return, spanning from c. 605/604 BC to 536/535 BC. The exact number of Sabbath years is 490 years, the period from Saul to the Babylonian captivity. This was retribution for their violation of the Sabbath law (see Leviticus 26:34–35; 2 Chronicles 36:21).

13. CONCERNING ALL THE NATIONS: Jeremiah prophesied judgments on surrounding nations (see chapters 46–49), while Babylon is the focus of judgment in chapters 50 and 51.

14. BE SERVED BY THEM: The Babylonians, who made other nations their slaves, would become the servants of nations.

15. THIS WINE CUP: A symbol for stupefying judgments (see Jeremiah 25:16).

17. ALL THE NATIONS DRINK: Obviously Jeremiah could not visit all the places listed from verses 18–26, but in this vision, he acted as if representatives from all those nations were present so he could make them drink in the message of wrath (see verse 27) and understand there was no escape (see verses 28–29).

29. BRING CALAMITY ON THE CITY . . . CALLED BY MY NAME: This refers to Jerusalem (see Daniel 9:18).

30–33. PROPHESY AGAINST THEM: While embracing the judgments soon to come to Judah and other nations, this has end-time language ("one end of the earth . . . to the other") and must be ultimately fulfilled in the time of tribulation described in Revelation 6–19.

JEREMIAH'S TWELFTH MESSAGE: Jeremiah delivers his twelfth message against Judah (26:1–24) at the beginning of Jehoiakim's reign, around 609 BC.

26:1. BEGINNING OF THE REIGN OF JEHOIAKIM: This message from Jeremiah was delivered about four years earlier than the one in 25:1 and about eleven years before the one in 24:1.

2. STAND IN THE COURT OF THE LORD'S HOUSE: This was the largest public gathering place at the temple.

6. SHILOH: The former dwelling place of God. See note on 7:12.

11. DESERVES TO DIE: Jeremiah was accused of treason. (See Paul's arrest in Acts 21:27–28.)

12. JEREMIAH SPOKE: The leaders and people had threatened to kill Jeremiah (see verse 8), so here the prophet defended himself while in extreme danger. He did not compromise but displayed great spiritual courage. He was ready to die (see verse 14) yet warned the crowd that God would hold the guilty accountable (see verse 15).

15. PUT ME TO DEATH: See Matthew 23:31–37.

17–19. ELDERS . . . SPOKE: These spokesmen cited the prophet Micah (see Micah 3:12), who before and during Hezekiah's reign (c. 715–686 BC) prophesied the destruction of Jerusalem and its temple. They reasoned that because they didn't kill Micah, God rescinded the judgment. For this same reason, they must not kill Jeremiah so that God might change His mind. Micah's prophecy and Jeremiah's would come true in time.

20–22. ALSO A MAN . . . PROPHESIED: Urijah, like Micah and Jeremiah, had warned of doom on Jerusalem, speaking in Jehoiakim's day only a bit earlier than Jeremiah's present warning (609 BC). He was executed. The decision could have gone either way, since there was precedent for killing and for sparing.

22. ELNATHAN: A high-ranking official who, on another occasion, sided with Jeremiah (see Jeremiah 36:12, 25).

23. THE GRAVES OF THE COMMON PEOPLE: In the Kidron Valley, to the east of the temple (see 2 Kings 23:6).

24. AHIKAM: He used his strategic influence to release Jeremiah from the death threat. This civil leader under King Josiah (see 2 Kings 22:12, 14), and father of Gedaliah, was appointed governor over Judah by the Babylonians after Jerusalem's final fall in 586 BC (see Jeremiah 39:14; 40:13–41:3).

JEREMIAH'S THIRTEENTH MESSAGE: Jeremiah delivers his thirteenth message against Judah (27:1–28:17) also at the beginning of Jehoiakim's reign (see verse 1). However, the correct reading might be Zedekiah (as in verses 3, 12, and 28:1), which would put the date at the outset of his 597–586 BC reign.

27:2. MAKE . . . BONDS AND YOKES: This object lesson symbolized bondage to Babylon. The yoke was placed on Jeremiah's neck to picture Judah's captivity (see verse 12) and then sent to six kings of nearby nations who would also be under Babylon's power (see verse 3). See also Jeremiah 28:10–12.

7. MANY NATIONS AND GREAT KINGS: See Jeremiah 25:13–14.

8. YOKE OF . . . BABYLON: The point of the object lesson is simple. Any nation that will serve Babylon willingly may stay in their own land, but nations that will not submit voluntarily to Babylon will suffer destruction. Consequently, Judah should submit and not be removed from the land (see verses 9–18).

18. MAKE INTERCESSION TO THE LORD OF HOSTS: God would not answer such a prayer, as proven by verses 19–22. This revealed His indifference to the prayers of these false prophets.

20. NEBUCHADNEZZAR . . . CARRIED AWAY CAPTIVE JECONIAH: c. 597 BC.

21–22. VESSELS: Jeremiah revealed that Judah's temple vessels taken to Babylon (see 2 Kings 24:13; Daniel 1:1–2) would be restored to the temple. Fulfillment around 536 BC was spoken of in Ezra 5:13–15. About 516/515 BC, these articles were placed in the rebuilt temple (see Ezra 6:15).

28:1. REIGN OF ZEDEKIAH: See note on Jeremiah 27:1. The fourth year would be about 593 BC.

HANANIAH: This man was one of several by this name in Scripture; in this case, he was a foe of God's true prophet, distinct from the loyal Hananiah of Daniel 1:6.

2–3. I HAVE BROKEN THE YOKE: The false prophet, of the kind Jeremiah warned in 27:14–16, predicted victory over Babylon and the return of the temple vessels within two years. In actuality, Babylon achieved its third and conclusive victory in conquering Judah eleven years later (586 BC) as in chapters 39, 40, 52. As to the vessels, see note on 27:21–22.

4. BRING BACK . . . JECONIAH: This rash, false claim fell into ignominy. Jeconiah, soon taken to Babylon in 597 BC, would live out his years there and not return to Jerusalem (see 52:31–34). Other captives either died in captivity or didn't return until sixty-one years later (see 22:24–26).

10. TOOK THE YOKE OFF: The phony prophet, in foolishness, removed the object lesson from the true spokesman and broke it as a sign of his own prediction coming true (see verses 2–4, 11).

13. GO AND TELL HANANIAH: Jeremiah apparently left the meeting; later, God sent him back to confront the liar, likely wearing yokes of iron (which Hananiah could not break!) to replace the wooden ones (see verse 14) and to illustrate his message.

15–17. THE LORD HAS NOT SENT YOU: Jeremiah told three things to Hananiah: (1) God had not approved his message; (2) he was guilty of encouraging the people to trust in a lie, even rebellion; and (3) God would require his life that very year, 597 BC. The true prophet's word was authenticated by Hananiah's death two months later (see verse 17).

> *JEREMIAH'S FOURTEENTH MESSAGE: Jeremiah addresses his fourteenth message (29:1–32) to his countrymen who had been deported to Babylon shortly after 597 BC. His words, recorded in a letter, were meant to comfort them in their exile.*

29:4–10. THUS SAYS THE LORD OF HOSTS: The prophet Jeremiah's counsel to the Israelites in Babylon was to live as colonists, planning to be there for a long time (seventy years; see verse 10). Further, they were to seek Babylon's peace and intercede in prayer for it, their own welfare being bound with it (see verse 7; see also Ezra 6:10; 7:23).

11. THOUGHTS OF PEACE: This assured God's intentions to bring about blessing in Israel's future (see chapters 30–33).

12–14. YOU WILL CALL UPON ME: What God planned, He also gave the people opportunity to participate in through sincere prayer (see verse 13; see also 1 John 5:14–15).

14. I WILL BE FOUND BY YOU: The Lord would answer the people's prayer by returning the Jews to their land. (See Daniel's example and God's response in Daniel 9:4–27.) Fulfillment would occur in the era of Ezra and Nehemiah, and beyond this time in even fuller measure after the Second Advent of their Messiah (see Daniel 2:35, 45; 7:13–14, 27; 12:1–3, 13).

15–19. BECAUSE YOU HAVE SAID: Still rejecting God's true message, Jewish captives listened to false prophets among them (see verses 8–9, 21–23). This was the very sin that would cause God to send a further deportation to those still in Judah (586 BC).

17. LIKE ROTTEN FIGS: See note on Jeremiah 24:8–10.

21–23. AHAB . . . AND ZEDEKIAH: Two captive, false Israelite prophets, who had been misleading exiles in Babylon (see verse 15), will stir up the wrath of their captor king, who will cast them into a furnace (as in Daniel 3). They aroused not only the Babylonian potentate's enmity but God's also, because of prophecies against His word and physical adultery (see Jeremiah 5:7).

24–32. SHEMAIAH THE NEHELAMITE: The judgment against Shemaiah, the otherwise unknown prophet who opposed Jeremiah, was similar to that experienced by Hananiah (see 28:15–17).

28. SENT TO US IN BABYLON: This referred to Jeremiah's letter mentioned in verse 5.

UNLEASHING THE TEXT

1) What charge did God make against the people of Judah in Jeremiah 25:1–7? What did He reveal about the nature of His judgment and how long it would last in verses 8–14?

_____

_____

_____

_____

2) Chapter 26 describes a life-threatening situation for Jeremiah. What are some reasons why his prophetic messages were so distasteful to the people of Judah?

_____

_____

_____

_____

3) What did the false prophet Hananiah declare about Judah's future in Jeremiah 28:1–4? How did Jeremiah respond to his words in verses 5–9?

_____

_____

_____

_____

4) How would you summarize God's message in Jeremiah 29 to the Jewish captives in Babylon? What specific instructions did He give them?

_____

_____

_____

_____

EXPLORING THE MEANING

Jeremiah was specific with his prophecy. As mentioned previously, Jeremiah was not the only prophet operating in Judah. There were many others who proclaimed themselves to be prophets yet did not speak the word of the Lord. Instead, they gained popularity and influence by telling the people—especially the religious and political leaders in Jerusalem—whatever they wanted to hear. One of the hallmarks of these false prophets was that they tended to be vague in their prophecies so as not to reveal details that could later be proven false. In Jeremiah's words, they declared "'Peace, peace!' when there is no peace" (8:11). Jeremiah, on the other hand, was specific in his prophecies. For example, he declared it was Nebuchadnezzar who would ultimately conquer Judah (see 25:8–11). Moreover, Jeremiah prophesied that a period of seventy years would pass between the Jewish captives being taken to Babylon and their release to rebuild Jerusalem (see verses 12–14). Jeremiah was not afraid to be specific in outlining the future because his information did not come from himself but from God.

Jeremiah was accurate with his prophecy. Because Jeremiah spoke only the word of the Lord, his prophecies are confirmed by history as being accurate—while the predictions of the false prophets were proven wrong. Chapters 27 and 28 offer an interesting window into that reality when Jeremiah was confronted by a false prophet named Hananiah. This was early in Jeremiah's ministry, and it started when God commanded Jeremiah to wear a yoke symbolizing Judah's conquest at the hands of Babylon. Jeremiah also sent yokes to the kings of other nations that Babylon had conquered or would conquer. The message was not subtle: God was revealing Judah's future subservience to Babylon. The Lord then said, "Do not listen to your prophets, your diviners, your dreamers, your soothsayers, or your sorcerers, who speak to you, saying, 'You shall not serve the king of Babylon.' For they prophesy a lie to you, to remove you far from your land; and I will drive you out, and you will perish" (27:9–10). Hananiah responded by removing Jeremiah's yoke and breaking it, declaring that God would break Babylon's dominance over Judah in like manner. God responded by declaring, through Jeremiah, that Hananiah would die within a year—a prophecy that came true. Jeremiah confirmed his status as God's prophet because his prophecies were consistently accurate.

Jeremiah was compassionate in his prophecy. We tend to think of Old Testament prophecies as consisting of only doom, gloom, and judgment. In Jeremiah's case, that stereotype is largely accurate. Much of what Jeremiah prophesied to the people of Judah *was* bad news—but not everything. Chapter 29 contains a long letter written by Jeremiah to those who had already been taken captive into Babylon. This letter was likely written in 597 BC, which means two waves of captives had been removed from Judah and relocated to Babylon. Jeremiah's letter was largely compassionate, offering God's declaration that those captives should make an effort to flourish while there in Babylon—"that you may be increased there, and not diminished" (verse 6). It would have been easy for those captives to believe their lives had lost meaning and purpose and that the nation of Israel itself would soon be finished. But God reassured His people and offered them hope even in that foreign land: "After seventy years are completed at Babylon, I will visit you and perform My good word toward you, and cause you to return to this place. For I know the thoughts that I think toward you, says the LORD, thoughts of peace and not of evil, to give you a future and a hope" (verses 10–11).

REFLECTING ON THE TEXT

5) What are some ways that Christians today can benefit from studying and contemplating biblical prophecy? How does such prophecy help us now?

_____

_____

_____

_____

6) In what ways has the Bible proven to be reliable and accurate in your life?

_____

_____

_____

_____

7) Why is it so critical to know how to discern between those who speak the truth about God's Word and those who simply tell others what they want to hear?

_____

_____

_____

_____

8) Look again at Jeremiah's letter to the captives in chapter 29. How does that letter apply to you?

_____

_____

_____

_____

_____

_____

PERSONAL RESPONSE

9) What problems have you encountered in your efforts to study Scripture? What is one step you could take today to address one of those issues?

_____

_____

_____

_____

_____

_____

10) Who is someone in your life who could use a "letter" or word of encouragement from you? What could you do today to touch that person's life with God's hope?

_____

_____

_____

_____

_____

7

A FORECAST OF RESTORATION

Jeremiah 30:1–33:26

DRAWING NEAR

What are some goals you would like to achieve in your spiritual life over the next five years? What about over the next twenty-five years?

_____

_____

_____

_____

_____

_____

_____

_____

_____

_____

_____

THE CONTEXT

God's words to Jeremiah in the opening verses of chapter 30 represent a turning point in the prophet's recorded messages: "Behold, the days are coming . . . that I will bring back from captivity My people Israel and Judah" (verse 3). In the previous lesson, we saw how God promised that His people's exile in Babylon would last only seventy years. After that time, God would gather His people in Jerusalem and empower them to rebuild its walls and temple.

At this point, the focus of Jeremiah's narrative in his book shifts in two major ways. First, the messages grouped together in this section (especially chapters 30–33) move away from God's judgment and instead emphasize His compassion and consolation. The prophet's words here are in many ways brimming with hope. Second, Jeremiah's prophecies shift from the short-term future to the long-term future—even to events that still have yet to occur. Chapters 30–33 speak not only of the future restoration of Jerusalem and the temple but also of a New Covenant that God would make with His people and of the coming Messiah.

This is particularly revealed in the following passage from Jeremiah: "But this is the covenant that I will make with the house of Israel after those days, says the LORD: I will put My law in their minds, and write it on their hearts; and I will be their God, and they shall be My people. . . . For I will forgive their iniquity, and their sin I will remember no more" (31:33–34).

KEYS TO THE TEXT

Read Jeremiah 30:1–33:26, noting the key words and phrases indicated below.

> A FORECAST OF RESTORATION: *Jeremiah, having concluded his fourteen messages against Judah, now prophesizes God's restoration of the nation after their exile.*

30:3. I WILL BRING BACK: This theme verse gives in capsule form the pledge of chapters 30–33. God's restoration of the nation to their own land (see Jeremiah 29:10; Amos 9:14–15; Romans 11:26) has in view a final regathering never to be removed again (see note on Jeremiah 16:15) and not just a return in the time of Ezra and Nehemiah (see verses 8–9; 31:31ff.; 32:39, 40; 33:8–9, 15–16). This verse is a summary of the prophecy given in verses 4–9.

7. TIME OF JACOB'S TROUBLE: This period of unprecedented difficulty for Israel, as the verse defines, is set in a context of Israel's final restoration. It is best equated with the time of tribulation (see verses 8–9) just before Christ's Second Advent, mentioned elsewhere (see Daniel 12:1; Matthew 24:21–22), and described in detail in Revelation 6–19.

9. DAVID THEIR KING: The Messiah—the greater David in David's dynasty—will ultimately fulfill this promise (see 2 Samuel 7:16). He is the great King often promised as Israel's hope (see Jeremiah 23:5–6; Isaiah 9:7; Ezekiel 37:24–25; Daniel 2:35, 45; 7:13–14, 27; Matthew 25:34; 26:64; Luke 1:32; Revelation 17:14;

19:16). No king of David's seed has held the scepter since the captivity. Zerubbabel, of David's line, never claimed the title of king (see Haggai 2:2).

10–11. NOT MAKE A COMPLETE END OF YOU: Israel will endure as a people until Messiah's kingdom (see Romans 11:1–29).

12–15. NO ONE TO PLEAD YOUR CAUSE: Judah had no reason to complain because their own sins brought God's judgment (see verse 15).

16–24. THEREFORE ALL THOSE WHO DEVOUR YOU SHALL BE DEVOURED: These absolute and extensive promises have yet to be fulfilled in history; they look forward to the reign of Christ, the greater David, in the millennial kingdom of the "latter days."

21. THEIR GOVERNOR SHALL COME FROM THEIR MIDST: This refers to the Messiah, the King of verse 9 and 23:5–6, springing up from within Israel (see Isaiah 11:1), able to approach God as a priest.

31:1. AT THE SAME TIME: A time to be equated with the latter days in 30:24. In this chapter, prophecies of the restoration of the nation are continued.

2–14. THUS SAYS THE LORD: The Lord describes the future messianic kingdom conditions.

15. A VOICE . . . IN RAMAH: The reflection, for a moment, is on the distress of an Israelite mother for her children killed in the Babylonian invasion. This was a backdrop for the many contrasting promises of restoration to a joyful time (as in verses 12–14, 16–17) in the messianic day. Matthew saw the same description of sadness as apt, in principle, to depict something of the similar weeping of Jewish mothers when King Herod had babies murdered at Bethlehem in a bid to destroy the Messiah as a child (see Matthew 2:17–18).

18–20. RESTORE ME: Jeremiah wrote of Israel (the ten tribes called Ephraim) as finally recognizing, in humility, the need for the Lord to move them to repentance and forgiveness. See Psalm 102:13–17 for the relation of Israel's restoration to their prayers (see also Jeremiah 24:6–7; Lamentations 5:21; John 6:44, 65).

22. BACKSLIDING: See note on Jeremiah 2:19.

A WOMAN SHALL ENCOMPASS A MAN: This is one of the most puzzling statements in Jeremiah. Some see the virgin birth of Christ in this statement, though "woman" means a woman, not a virgin, and "encompass" or "surround" does not suggest conceiving. Possibly, the words refer to the formerly virgin Israel (see verse 21), who is now a disgraced, divorced wife (see verse 22; 3:8). She will one day in the future reembrace her former husband, the Lord, and He will receive her back, fully forgiven. That would be "a new thing on the earth."

26. MY SLEEP WAS SWEET: The hope of Israel's restoration brought a moment of peace in Jeremiah's otherwise tumultuous ministry.

28. BUILD AND . . . PLANT: The Lord repeated what He at first told Jeremiah in 1:10 regarding His two works of judging and blessing. The latter is described with two images: architectural (building) and agricultural (planting).

29. SOUR GRAPES: This was apparently a proverb among the exiles' children born in Babylon to express the fact that they suffered the consequences of their fathers' sins rather than their own (see Lamentations 5:7; Ezekiel 18:2–3).

31–34. A NEW COVENANT: In contrast to the Mosaic covenant under which Israel failed, God promised a New Covenant with a spiritual, divine dynamic by which those who know Him would participate in the blessings of salvation. The fulfillment was to individuals, yet also to Israel as a nation (see verse 36; Romans 11:16–27). It is set (1) in the framework of a reestablishment of the nation in their land (for example, chapters 30–33 and in verses 38–40), and (2) in the time after the ultimate difficulty (see 30:7). In principle, this covenant, also announced by Jesus Christ (see Luke 22:20), begins to be fulfilled spiritually by Jewish and Gentile believers in the church era (see 1 Corinthians 11:25; 2 Corinthians 3:6; Hebrews 8:7–13; 9:15; 10:14–17; 12:24; 13:20). It has already begun to take effect with "the remnant according to the election of grace" (Romans 11:5). It will be also realized by the people of Israel in the last days, including the regathering to their ancient land, Palestine (see chapters 30–33). The streams of the Abrahamic, Davidic, and New Covenants find their confluence in the millennial kingdom ruled by the Messiah.

35–37. THE LORD, WHO GIVES THE SUN FOR A LIGHT: These verses emphasize the certainty with which Israel can expect God to fulfill the New Covenant (see 33:17–22, 25–26).

38. THE CITY SHALL BE BUILT FOR THE LORD: When New Covenant promises are ultimately fulfilled in Israel's regathering to her land, rebuilt Jerusalem will meet certain specifications.

TOWER OF HANANEL: The tower was in the northeast corner of the city (see Nehemiah 3:1; 12:39).

CORNER GATE: The Corner Gate was at the northwest corner (2 Kings 14:13; 2 Chronicles 26:9).

39. SURVEYOR'S LINE: The "surveyor's line" marked out the area for rebuilding. It would point over the hill Gareb and then toward Goath; both places are impossible to identify today.

40. VALLEY OF THE DEAD BODIES: The valley of Hinnom, a place of refuse and burning fires (see note on Jeremiah 7:31).

HORSE GATE: The Horse Gate was at the southeast corner of the temple courts (see 2 Kings 11:16; Nehemiah 3:28).

THE FAITH IN RESTORATION: Jeremiah delivers this next prophecy from a prison in 587 BC, the tenth year in Zedekiah's reign (597–586 BC) and eighteenth of Nebuchadnezzar's rule, during Babylon's siege of Jerusalem.

32:2. BABYLON'S ARMY BESIEGED: The siege, set up in the tenth month (January) of 588 BC, lasted at least thirty months, to the fourth month (July) of 586 BC (see note on Jeremiah 34:1). The events of the chapter occurred in this setting of Judah's imminent loss of her land, only about a year before Babylon's final takeover detailed in chapters 39–40 and 52.

2–5. SHUT UP IN ... PRISON: Judah's final king put Jeremiah into prison on the charge of preaching treason against both nation and king, whereas Zedekiah savored positive talk to spark new resolve to hold out against the Babylonians.

8. THE RIGHT OF INHERITANCE: A man facing hardship could sell property, and the right to redeem it until the Jubilee year belonged to the closest blood relative. If a stranger had taken it due to unpaid debt, the relative could redeem it as a family possession (see Leviticus 25:25). Levite land could be sold only to a Levite (see Leviticus 25:32–34), such as Jeremiah. He did as the Lord told him (see Jeremiah 32:9–12).

14. TAKE THESE DEEDS: Title deeds to the land, kept for security reasons in a pottery jar, would attest in a future day to one's claim of possession. Men of Anathoth did return to Jerusalem from Babylon (see Ezra 2:23). Also, some of the poor of the land, left by the Babylonians (see chapter 39), could have included certain inhabitants of Anathoth. In a still future day, God will be able (see Jeremiah 32:17, 27) to return this land to a resurrected Jeremiah and confirm to the right people that they are the prophet/priest's descendants.

16–25. WHEN I HAD DELIVERED THE PURCHASE DEED: With the immense sovereign power God has to do whatever He wishes in the present captivity and the future return, Jeremiah wondered why God had him redeem the field.

26–35. INTO THE HAND OF THE CHALDEANS: God reviewed Judah's sins and affirmed to Jeremiah that the Babylonians would prevail over Jerusalem (see "this city" in verse 28).

36–41. I WILL GATHER THEM: However, one day God will restore Israel to the land and provide the blessing of salvation.

37. BRING THEM BACK: God pledged to restore the people to the very land of Israel (see verse 44). It is natural to expect His fulfillment of this blessing to be just as literal as the reverse—His scattering from the land (see verse 42).

38–39. THEY SHALL BE MY PEOPLE: This speaks of spiritual salvation; that is, the true knowledge and worship of God.

40. AN EVERLASTING COVENANT: The ultimate fulfillment of a future in the land was not fulfilled in the Ezra/Nehemiah return. This occurs in the time when God gives the people of Israel a new heart in eternal salvation along with their return to the ancient land (see Jeremiah 33:8–9; Ezekiel 36:26).

42–44. SO I WILL BRING ON THEM ALL THE GOOD: In the millennial kingdom, land will again be bought and sold in Israel.

A FURTHER FORECAST OF RESTORATION: The word of the Lord comes to Jeremiah a second time while he is in prison under King Zedekiah.

33:3. CALL . . . I WILL ANSWER: God invited Jeremiah's prayer, which the prophet appealed to Him to fulfill the aspects of His promises that He guaranteed to keep (as in Jeremiah 29:11–14; Daniel 9:4–19; see also John 15:7). His answer to the prayer was assured in verses 4–26 (see also verse 14).

6. TRUTH: Truth conforms to a standard—either to created reality or to God's standards. Truth is often associated with mercy, especially God's mercy (see Genesis 24:49; Psalms 57:3; 117:2). This word is also frequently used in the context of legal language. In secular contexts, it is used in speaking of witnesses and judgments (see Proverbs 14:25; Zechariah 8:16), while in the religious contexts it is used in reference to the law and commandments of God (see Psalm 119:142, 151). Truth is precious, and its absence was lamented by the prophets (see Jeremiah 9:5; Isaiah 59:14; Hosea 4:1). God desires truth in the inward parts of His people (see Psalms 15:2; 51:6); thus, it is the basis of a lifestyle that pleases Him (see Psalms 25:5, 10; 26:3).

8. CLEANSE THEM FROM ALL THEIR INIQUITY: Again, the Lord emphasized the individual spiritual salvation associated with the New Covenant restoration to the land.

11. PRAISE THE LORD: These are the words of Psalm 136:1, actually used by the Jews on their return from Babylon (see Ezra 3:11).

15. A BRANCH OF RIGHTEOUSNESS: This is the Messiah King in David's lineage, as in Jeremiah 23:5–6. He is the King whose reign immediately follows the second coming when He appears in power (see Daniel 2:35, 45; 7:13–14, 27; Matthew 16:27–28; 24:30; 26:64).

17–22. DAVID SHALL NEVER LACK: God promised to fulfill the Davidic (see 2 Samuel 17) and priestly (see Numbers 25:10–13) covenants without exception. The promise was as certain as the sure appearance of night and day and the incalculable number of stars or sand grains (see Jeremiah 31:35–37; 33:25–26).

24. TWO FAMILIES: Judah and Israel.

HE HAS ALSO CAST THEM OFF: Many people, even today, believe that Israel as a nation has no future. In verses 25–26, God emphatically denies that notion (see also Jeremiah 31:35–36; Psalm 74:16–17; Romans 11:1–2). God will restore the nation.

UNLEASHING THE TEXT

1) What is God's promise to His people in Jeremiah 30:3? How does this verse look past the immediate period of their exile to a future not-yet-fulfilled event?

_____

_____

_____

2) What does the Lord say in Jeremiah 31:31–34 about the New Covenant that He will bring?

_____

_____

_____

3) How would you summarize the point of God telling Jeremiah to buy a field in chapter 32?

_____

_____

_____

_____

4) What encouragement do you gain from God's words in Jeremiah 33:3?

_____

_____

_____

_____

EXPLORING THE MEANING

God's words promised hope. At the beginning of chapter 30, God changed the tone of His words spoken to His people through the prophet Jeremiah: "Thus speaks the LORD God of Israel, saying: 'Write in a book for yourself all the words that I have spoken to you. . . . I will bring back from captivity My people Israel and Judah. . . . And I will cause them to return to the land that I gave to their fathers, and they shall possess it'" (verses 2–3). As mentioned previously, the prophecies in the book of Jeremiah up to this point are generally negative—primarily declarations of God's judgment and wrath. Importantly, the Lord did *not* renounce those prophecies. The destruction of Jerusalem was still imminent, yet God would not abandon His people. After seventy years of captivity, He would bring them back. Not only that, God promised to bless His people: "Then out of them shall proceed thanksgiving and the voice of those who make merry; I will multiply them, and they shall not diminish; I will also glorify them, and they shall not be small" (30:19). These were words of hope in advance of suffering.

God's covenant promised hope. For generations, the Jewish people had experienced their relationship with God through a series of covenants—primarily the Abrahamic Covenant (see Genesis 12:1–3), the Mosaic Covenant (see Deuteronomy 11:1–32), and the Davidic Covenant (see 2 Samuel 7:8–16). These legal measures provided the expectations for Israel's existence as God's chosen people. Imagine the shock, then, when God spoke these words through Jeremiah: "Behold, the days are coming, says the LORD, when I will make a new covenant with the house of Israel and with the house of Judah. . . . But this is the covenant that I will make with the house of Israel after those days, says the LORD: I will put My law in their minds, and write it on their hearts; and I will be their God, and they shall be My people" (Jeremiah 31:31, 33). This promise of a New Covenant was ultimately fulfilled through the life and death of Jesus, as He Himself declared: "Likewise He also took the cup after supper, saying, 'This cup is the new covenant in My blood, which is shed for you'" (Luke 22:20). On the verge of destruction and disaster, God's promise of a future New Covenant was a lifeline of hope.

Jeremiah's actions promised hope. In many ways, 587 BC was the low point of Judah's history as a nation. Jerusalem had been under siege for more than two years by that point, and the population was hungry and desperate. Everyone could see that the Babylonians were close to their goal of total conquest and complete destruction. In that moment, when Jeremiah was "shut up" as a prisoner in the king's house, he received a visit from a relative who made a strange request: "Please buy my field that is in Anathoth, which is in the country of Benjamin; for the right of inheritance is yours, and the redemption yours; buy it for yourself" (Jeremiah 32:8). Remember, the entire nation was on the cusp of becoming Babylonian territory. Real estate was not a good investment! However, God told Jeremiah to accept his relative's request and buy the field as a sign of hope for His people: "Behold, I will gather them out of all countries where I have driven them in My anger, in My fury, and in great wrath; I will bring them back to this place, and I will cause them to dwell safely" (verse 37). When the seventy years of captivity were concluded, the Israelites would return to their promised land.

REFLECTING ON THE TEXT

5) What does the fact that God was willing to restore the people of Judah—after all the idolatry and evil they had committed—reveal about His character?

_____

_____

_____

_____

6) Jeremiah's words would have provided great hope to the people going into exile. What are some passages of Scripture that have provided hope for you during dark times?

_____

_____

_____

_____

7) God's covenants and His laws were written down for the people of Israel so that they would know His expectations for them as His chosen people. What would be different about the New Covenant that Jesus would ultimately bring (see Jeremiah 31:31–34)?

_____

_____

_____

_____

_____

_____

8) How does the gospel offer hope and salvation today for those in spiritual exile?

_____

_____

_____

_____

_____

PERSONAL RESPONSE

9) What is causing a loss or a lack of hope in your life right now?

_____

_____

_____

_____

_____

_____

10) Where do you have an opportunity to be a source of hope to someone who needs it?

_____

_____

_____

_____

_____

CALAMITY FORETOLD ON JUDAH

Jeremiah 34:1–39:18

DRAWING NEAR

Think of a recent time when you received some bad news. How did you handle that situation?

_____

_____

_____

_____

_____

_____

_____

_____

_____

_____

_____

_____

_____

_____

_____

_____

_____

_____

_____

_____

THE CONTEXT

Jeremiah served as a prophet for many decades and interacted with several different kings of Judah. As you will recall, he received his call from God during the thirteenth year of the reign of King Josiah (see Jeremiah 1:1–3). Josiah was a righteous king who repented of the wickedness and rebellion of his fathers and initiated many reforms. However, those reforms did not significantly change the hearts of God's people. They remained rebellious at the core.

After Josiah came King Jehoahaz, who reigned for three months before being taken in chains to Egypt (see 2 Kings 23:31–34). His son Eliakim, whom Pharaoh Necho renamed Jehoiakim, then reigned for eleven years (see verses 34–37). During that time, he became a vassal of Nebuchadnezzar (see 24:1). Next came Jeconiah (or Jehoiachin), who reigned for three months before being carried off to Babylon during the second wave of captives (see verses 8–12). He was replaced by Zedekiah, who tried to throw off the yoke of Babylon, which resulted in the final siege and destruction of Jerusalem in 586 BC (see 24:16–25:11).

Each of these kings mentioned in Jeremiah's prophecies contributed to the downward spiritual trajectory of Judah. Many of them not only failed to heed Jeremiah's warnings but also attacked the prophet for declaring God's pronouncement of imminent doom. Jeremiah 34–39 includes content that spans the early years of King Jehoiakim (likely around 605 BC) all the way up to the fall and destruction of Jerusalem. In compiling these chapters, Jeremiah placed these events from different timelines together to emphasize specific themes—for instance, to show how the obedience of the Rechabites (a semi-nomadic people group) contrasted with the general disobedience of Judah's leaders (see chapter 35). Chapter 39 describes the climax of Jeremiah's story in terms of its narrative arc: the destruction of Jerusalem.

KEYS TO THE TEXT

Read Jeremiah 34:1–39:18, noting the key words and phrases indicated below.

> ZEDEKIAH WARNED: *This chapter is set in Zedekiah's reign, during the siege of Jerusalem in 588–586 BC, and is an amplification of Jeremiah 32:1–5—the message that resulted in Jeremiah's incarceration.*

34:1. NEBUCHADNEZZAR . . . FOUGHT: The Babylonian siege began c. January 15, 588 BC (see Jeremiah 39:1) and ended c. July 18, 586 (see 39:2; 52:5–6).

AGAINST JERUSALEM: Babylon's destruction of Jerusalem began August 14, 586 BC (see 2 Kings 25:8–9).

3. YOU SHALL NOT ESCAPE: This prophecy about Zedekiah (see also 32:1–5) was fulfilled as reported in 2 Kings 25:6–7 and Jeremiah 52:7–11.

8–10. A COVENANT . . . TO PROCLAIM LIBERTY: Zedekiah's pact to free slaves met with initial compliance. The covenant followed the law of release (see Leviticus 25:39–55; Deuteronomy 15:12–18) in hopes of courting God's favor and ending His judgment.

11. THEY CHANGED THEIR MINDS: Former slave masters went back on their agreement and recalled the slaves. Some suggest that this treachery came when the inhabitants believed that the danger was past, because the Egyptian army approached and Babylon's forces withdrew temporarily (see Jeremiah 37:5, 11).

12–16. THEREFORE THE WORD OF THE LORD CAME TO JEREMIAH: God reminded the unfaithful Jews of His own covenant, when He freed Israelites from Egyptian bondage (see Exodus 21:2; Deuteronomy 15:12–15). He had commanded that Hebrew slaves should serve only six years, being set free in the seventh (see Jeremiah 34:13–14).

17–22. YOU HAVE NOT OBEYED: Due to recent duplicity (see verse 16), God promised only one kind of liberty to the offenders: liberty to judgment by sword, pestilence, and famine (see verse 17).

18–21. CUT THE CALF IN TWO: God would give the guilty over to death before the conqueror, for they had denied the covenant ratified by blood (see verse 21). In this custom, as in Genesis 15:8–17, two parties laid out parts of a sacrifice on two sides and then walked between the parts. By that symbolic action, each person pledged to fulfill his promise, agreeing in effect, "May my life (represented by the blood) be poured out if I fail to honor my part."

THE OBEDIENT RECHABITES: *This chapter provides a description of the commitment to obedience by a group of people to their father, in contrast to the Jews' disobedience of God.*

35:1. DAYS OF JEHOIAKIM: The setting is 609–597 BC. This looks back to several years before Jeremiah 34:1, possibly for a thematic reason—to cite a case of obedience after the episode of treachery in chapter 34.

2. THE RECHABITES: These were a semi-nomadic, Kenite group, related to Moses' father-in-law (see Judges 1:16; 4:11), descended from those in

1 Chronicles 2:55. The originator of their customs was Jonadab (see Jeremiah 35:6, 14; 2 Kings 10:15, 23). They derived their name from Rechab (see Jeremiah 35:8) and were not of Jacob's seed but "strangers" in Israel.

8. WE HAVE OBEYED: What was commended here was not the father's specific commands about nomadic life but the steadfast obedience of the sons. Their obedience was unreserved in all aspects, at all times, on the part of all, without exception; in all these respects, Israel was lacking (see verse 14).

13–17. WILL YOU NOT RECEIVE INSTRUCTION: The prophet indicted the Jews for their flagrant disobedience against God.

18–19. BECAUSE YOU HAVE OBEYED: God would bless the Rechabites not in spiritually saving them all but in preserving a posterity in which some could have a place in His service. A Rechabite still had a role in Nehemiah 3:14. Also, the title over Psalm 71 in the Septuagint was addressed for use by the sons of Jonadab and the earliest captives.

THE SCROLL READ IN THE TEMPLE: *The setting for this chapter goes back several years earlier than chapters 32–34, before or shortly after the first of three deportations from Jerusalem to Babylon in 605 BC.*

36:2. TAKE A SCROLL . . . WRITE ON IT: The command to Jeremiah from the Lord was to record in one volume all the messages since the outset of Jeremiah's ministry in 627 BC (Jeremiah 1:2) up to 605/604 BC, to be read to the people in the temple (see verse 6).

4. BARUCH WROTE: Jeremiah's recording secretary (see 32:12) wrote the prophet's messages (see 45:1) and penned them a second time after the first scroll was burned (see 36:32). He also read the messages in the temple (see verse 10) and in the palace (see verse 15). Later, Jehudi read a small part of the first scroll before King Jehoiakim (see verses 21–23).

5. CONFINED: The word means "restricted, hindered, shut up" and is the same term used for imprisonment in 33:1; 39:15. The fact that princes allowed Jeremiah to depart into hiding (see 36:19) might indicate that he was curtailed in some ways without being in prison. There is no record of Jeremiah being imprisoned during Jehoiakim's rule.

6. THE DAY OF FASTING: See verse 9. Here was a special fast day, appointed to avert the impending calamity, that would make the Jews more open to the message of the prophet (see verse 7).

9. FIFTH YEAR: This year (604 BC) was the following year after that of verse 1, which may suggest that it took some part of a year to repeat and record the long series of messages that had so far been given (see verse 18).

NINTH MONTH: November/December (see verses 22–23).

10. IN THE CHAMBER OF GEMARIAH: Baruch read from a window or balcony on the north side, above the wall overlooking the temple court, where the people gathered.

17–18. DID YOU WRITE ALL THESE WORDS: The group who had gathered asked if Baruch had written these words from memory or actual dictation from the inspired prophet. The latter was true. They were concerned it might be God's Word (see verses 16, 25).

23. CUT IT: As often as Jehudi read "three or four columns," the king cut it up, doing so all the way through the whole scroll because he rejected the message (see verse 29). Jehoiakim is the king who sent men to Egypt (chapter 26) to bring back God's faithful prophet, Urijah, so he could execute him.

24. NOT AFRAID: The king's servants were more hardened than the princes.

26. THE LORD HID THEM: God, who guides (see 1:8, 19; 10:23), provided Jeremiah and Baruch with safety (see 36:19; Psalm 32:8; Proverbs 3:5–6).

27–28. TAKE YET ANOTHER SCROLL: See Isaiah 40:18; 55:11; Matthew 5:18.

30–31. I WILL PUNISH HIM: Consequences followed Jehoiakim's defiance. He died in 598 BC (see Jeremiah 22:18–19; 2 Kings 23:36; 2 Chronicles 36:5), but there were none to occupy the throne for long (see Jeremiah 36:30). His son Jehoiachin, also known as Jeconiah (Coniah in 22:24), did succeed him, but with virtually no rule at all, lasting only three months and ten days in 597 BC (see 22:24–30; 2 Chronicles 36:9–10). Babylon deported him for the rest of his life (see Jeremiah 52:31–34) and none of his descendants ruled (see 22:30).

> ZEDEKIAH'S VAIN HOPE: Zedekiah, an uncle of Jeconiah, was raised to the throne by Nebuchadnezzar in contempt for Jehoiakim and Jeconiah. His eleven-year vassal rule spanned from 597–586 BC. The message of the king to Jeremiah in this chapter is somewhat earlier than that in chapter 21, when Zedekiah was afraid of the Babylonians' defeat of Egypt and returning to besiege Jerusalem.

37:4. COMING AND GOING: The prophet was no longer in the prison court, as he had been (see Jeremiah 32:2; 33:1).

7–10. SAY TO THE KING: Babylon, which temporarily ended the siege to deal with an Egyptian advance, would return and destroy Jerusalem.

12. JEREMIAH WENT OUT: He returned to his hometown to claim the property he had purchased (see 32:6–12).

13. HANANIAH: Jeremiah had predicted his death (see 28:16), and thus the grandson took revenge with a false accusation (see 38:19; 52:15).

15. STRUCK HIM: Jeremiah often absorbed blows, threats, or other mistreatment for proclaiming the truth from God (see 11:21; 20:2; 26:8; 36:26; 38:6, 25).

17. IS THERE ANY WORD FROM THE LORD: This showed Zedekiah's willful rejection. He knew that Jeremiah spoke for God.

19. PROPHETS: Those prophets who said the "king of Babylon" would not come were shown to be liars. In fact, he had come and would return.

21. GIVE HIM DAILY . . . BREAD: The king showed a measure of kindness by returning Jeremiah to "the court of the prison" (see 32:2; 33:1), promising "bread" as long as it lasted during the siege (see 38:9). Jeremiah remained there until Jerusalem was taken soon after the food was gone (see 38:28), with only a brief trip to a pit (see 38:6–13).

38:4. LET THIS MAN BE PUT TO DEATH: See Jeremiah 26:11.

HE WEAKENS THE HANDS: The princes charged that Jeremiah's urging to submit to Babylon (see 38:2) undermined the defenders' morale and will. By proclaiming Babylon's victory, he was viewed as a traitor to Judah.

5. THE KING CAN DO NOTHING: This represents the spineless evasion of duty by a leader (Zedekiah) who rejected God's Word.

6. NO WATER, BUT MIRE: The murderous princes (see verse 4) would let God's spokesman die of thirst, hunger, hypothermia, or suffocation if he sank too deeply into the bottom of the cistern. (See Psalm 69:2, 14, which is a reference to Messiah.)

7–13. EBED-MELECH: An Ethiopian, Gentile stranger acted decisively to deliver Jeremiah from his own people who were seeking to kill him. Perhaps a keeper of the royal harem ("eunuch"), this man later received God's deliverance of his own life and His tribute for his faith (see Jeremiah 39:15–18).

14–23. I WILL ASK YOU: This is one of several queries; Zedekiah wanted to hear God's Word, but he rejected it. God's Word was for him to surrender, and His answer for Zedekiah's rejection was calamity for Jerusalem, capture of the king, and tragedy for his family plus others of the palace. For the fulfillment of this prophecy, see 39:4–8.

CALAMITY FORETOLD ON JUDAH

22. CLOSE FRIENDS HAVE SET UPON YOU: Palace women, taken over by Babylonians, heaped ridicule on Zedekiah for listening to friends whose counsel failed him. The king was left helpless, like a person with his feet stuck in mire.

27. THESE WORDS . . . THE KING . . . COMMANDED: Jeremiah did not fall into lying deception here. What he said was true, though he did not divulge all details of the conversation to which the princes had no right.

> THE FALL OF JERUSALEM: *During the siege of Jerusalem, the enemy surrounded the city walls, cut off all entrances and exits, and cut off all food supplies and as much water as possible so that famine, thirst, and disease would eventually weaken the beleaguered city dwellers and they could easily be conquered.*

39:1–2. NINTH YEAR . . . ELEVENTH YEAR: The Babylonian siege began c. January 15, 588 BC and lasted thirty months (see Jeremiah 52:1–7; 2 Kings 25:1–4).

3. SAT IN THE MIDDLE GATE: This expressed full military occupation of the city, since this gate was between the upper city (Mount Zion) and the lower city to the north.

5. RIBLAH IN . . . HAMATH: Nebuchadnezzar's command headquarters were located 230 miles north of Jerusalem.

PRONOUNCED JUDGMENT: Nebuchadnezzar dealt with King Zedekiah as if he were a common criminal. The king had violated his oath (see 2 Chronicles 36:13; Ezekiel 17:13–19).

6–7. MOREOVER HE PUT OUT ZEDEKIAH'S EYES: This reconciles Jeremiah 32:4 with Ezekiel 12:13.

8–10. BURNED THE KING'S HOUSE: See Jeremiah 52:12–16; 2 Kings 25:8–12.

11–12. CHARGE CONCERNING JEREMIAH: Jeremiah's prophecies were known to Nebuchadnezzar through defectors (see verse 9; 38:19), and also through Jews taken to Babylon with Jeconiah (see 40:2).

14. THEY SENT SOMEONE TO TAKE JEREMIAH FROM THE COURT: This was given as a general summary, whereas 40:1–6 contains more detail about Jeremiah being first carried to Ramah (see 40:1) with the other captives before being released (see 40:2–5). Gedaliah, a former supporter of Jeremiah (see 26:24) and chief among the defectors loyal to Nebuchadnezzar, was made governor over the remnant left in the land (see 40:5).

15–18. IN THE COURT OF THE PRISON: See Jeremiah 38:7–13.

UNLEASHING THE TEXT

1) As previously noted, the events that are depicted in Jeremiah 34–39 are pulled from different timelines to emphasize specific themes. What particular themes stood out to you?

_____

_____

_____

_____

_____

_____

_____

2) In Jeremiah 36, different people responded very differently to Jeremiah's scroll. What can we learn about those individuals based on their responses?

_____

_____

_____

_____

_____

_____

_____

3) What are your impressions of King Zedekiah based on chapters 37 and 38? What are some words that describe his character?

_____

_____

_____

_____

_____

_____

4) What happened to Jeremiah after the destruction of Jerusalem? Why do you think Nebuzaradan, the Babylonian captain of the guard, treated Jeremiah in that way (see 39:11–18)?

_____

_____

_____

_____

_____

_____

Exploring the Meaning

Two pictures of obedience. Jeremiah juxtaposed two events in his prophetic record as a way of highlighting the lack of obedience in Judah. The first was an oath taken by the people near the beginning of Nebuchadnezzar's final siege of Jerusalem. The people in the city committed to freeing their slaves, in accordance with Mosaic law (see Leviticus 25:39–55), but then changed their minds and put those who had been freed back into slavery (see Jeremiah 34:8–11). What happened? What caused such a drastic shift in behavior? A likely answer is that the people of Jerusalem changed their minds after Babylon briefly relented in its siege to deal with the armies of Egypt (see Jeremiah 37:6–10). Those who had freed their slaves likely believed their problems were at an end and decided to regain their slaves. By contrast, Jeremiah highlights a group known as the Rechabites—a nomadic people who were not of Jewish descent—who had made a covenant with its patriarch, Jonadab, to abstain from alcohol. They remained true to that oath even when Jeremiah the prophet urged them to take wine (see 35:1–11). Their obedience highlighted the disobedience of God's chosen people.

Two disobedient kings. In the fourth year of Jehoiakim's reign—about twenty years before the final destruction of Jerusalem—God told Jeremiah to record his prophecies on a scroll. Transcribed by Baruch, the scroll contained God's promises of judgment, captivity, and destruction against Judah if the people did not repent. When the scroll was read out loud, many of Judah's "princes" were alarmed. But after the king read it, he cut it up, burned it, and gave orders for Jeremiah and Baruch to be seized (though God hid them). Two decades later, Jeremiah was still preaching his message of judgment. However, by that time the prophet's words carried power, for the armies of Babylon had camped near the city and the threat of destruction was imminently near. King Zedekiah was not openly hostile toward Jeremiah, but neither did he hear and obey the Lord's counsel. He tried to play both sides—first imprisoning Jeremiah, then releasing him, then imprisoning him again, then seeking advice and counsel. What can we learn from these two troubled kings? Primarily that both failed to do what was right. They both failed to submit themselves to God's authority and instead trusted in their own resources. As a result, they brought great harm to themselves and their people.

Two different prisons. When Jeremiah went to the land of Benjamin to claim the field he had purchased from his relative, he was met there by the captain of the guard and accused of defecting to the Babylonians. As a result, King Zedekiah locked him in "the court of the prison" (Jeremiah 37:21), where he received a daily ration of bread. Some time later, the princes of the city demanded that Zedekiah put Jeremiah to death. Zedekiah's response was spineless and sniveling: "Look, he is in your hand. For the king can do nothing against you'" (38:5). As a result, Jeremiah was thrown into a deep cistern filled with mire. He "sank in the mire" (verse 6) and was left to die. Although he was eventually rescued, it was a terrifying ordeal. What is important to consider in each of these events is that Jeremiah was always God's servant—whether as a free man, in the court of the prison, or in the mire. His circumstances did not determine his faithfulness to God; rather, he obeyed the Lord and declared His message both in seasons of relative prosperity and seasons of suffering. We are called to do the same.

REFLECTING ON THE TEXT

5) Jeremiah juxtaposed the story of the people of Jerusalem's decision to take back their slaves with the example of the Rechabites. What point was he making about God's people?

----

6) Jeremiah had the opportunity to be released from his suffering in prison when he met secretly with Zedekiah (see 37:16–17). What did he do instead?

_____

_____

_____

_____

_____

7) When have you been blessed or vindicated because you stood firm in your trust of God?

_____

_____

_____

_____

_____

8) Jeremiah served God faithfully in both the good times and the bad. What does his example reveal about the kinds of people whom God uses for His service?

_____

_____

_____

_____

_____

PERSONAL RESPONSE

9) When have you recently disobeyed God or failed to follow through with His will? What would you do differently if you could face that situation again?

_____

_____

_____

_____

_____

10) Do you find it easy or difficult to trust God in your current season of life? Explain your response.

_____

_____

_____

_____

_____

_____

_____

_____

9

Prophecies to the Remnant
Jeremiah 40:1–48:47

Drawing Near

When have you been caught up in something that you knew was a bad idea? How did you remove yourself from that situation?

_____

_____

_____

_____

_____

_____

_____

_____

_____

_____

_____

_____

_____

The Context

For decades, Jeremiah had declared the word of the Lord that Judah and Jerusalem would receive judgment because of the people's rebellion against God and their infatuation with idolatry. Jeremiah had suffered greatly as a result of this steadfast resolve to speak only God's words and not give in to the temptation to tell those in power what they wanted to hear. But in spite of all Jeremiah's warnings, the people refused to repent and instead chose to believe the words of false prophets, to promised divine deliverance. This resulted in their destruction.

The previous lesson ended with the sack of Jerusalem and the capture of Zedekiah. The king of Judah had attempted to sneak out of the city by night with some of his men, but they were captured by the Babylonians in the plains of Jericho. Nebuchadnezzer then pronounced his judgment against Zedekiah, killing all his sons in front of him, gouging out his eyes, and taking him into exile. The armies of Babylon then devastated regions throughout Judah before besieging God's holy city (see Jeremiah 39:4–9). As we have seen, that siege lasted thirty months—more than two years of confusion, hunger, thirst, and constant fear. In the end, the walls around Jerusalem were torn down, and the temple was destroyed as well.

In this lesson, we will explore the aftermath of that event. While most of those who had taken refuge in Jerusalem were killed or carried away into captivity, a remnant were left behind to keep the city functioning. Specifically, a group of poor farmers and vinedressers remained to tend the crops and raise tribute for Babylon. Jeremiah was among this group. In addition to reviewing those events, we will also look at Jeremiah's prophecies against various nations, which were likely collected from different time periods over the course of his ministry.

KEYS TO THE TEXT

Read Jeremiah 40:1–48:47, noting the key words and phrases indicated below.

> JEREMIAH WITH GEDALIAH: *The events of this chapter occur after Jeremiah had been released by Nebuzaradan, the Babylonian captain of the guard.*

40:2–3. THE LORD YOUR GOD HAS PRONOUNCED THIS DOOM: The pagan captain understood the judgment of God better than the leaders of Judah.

4–5. GO WHEREVER IT SEEMS CONVENIENT FOR YOU TO GO: The captain did exactly as Nebuchadnezzar had instructed him to do in Jeremiah 39:12.

5–6. JEREMIAH WENT TO GEDALIAH: Jeremiah chose to go to Gedaliah, the newly appointed governor at Mizpah, located several miles north of Jerusalem. Gedaliah was soon to be assassinated (see 41:1–3).

7. ALL THE CAPTAINS . . . IN THE FIELDS: The leaders of Judah's army had scattered in fear.

9–12. SERVE THE KING OF BABYLON: God had tempered the severity of His judgment by allowing a remnant to prosper.

13–16. JOHANAN: His warning of Ishmael's death plot went unheeded.

41:1–4. ISHMAEL . . . CAME WITH TEN MEN: In the second month after the city of Jerusalem had been burned, the careless governor entertained Ishmael's group and invited a massacre.

5. EIGHTY MEN: Most likely, this group had come in mourning over the destruction of Jerusalem, and so servants (see verse 8) were led to slaughter. Ishmael did amazing damage with only ten men (see verse 1). Eventually, they must have acquired more men, in order to do what is described in verse 10.

9. ASA: He ruled Judah c. 911–873 BC. See 1 Kings 15:16–22.

12–15. WENT TO FIGHT WITH ISHMAEL: Johanan heard of Ishmael's murders and his taking people captive; thus, he brought men to stop him. They freed the captives (see verses 13–14), but Ishmael and his men escaped (see verse 15).

12. POOL . . . GIBEON: See 2 Samuel 2:13.

42:1–2. JOHANAN . . . SAID TO JEREMIAH: Jeremiah had probably been carried off from Mizpah, freed, and was now dwelling with Johanan (see Jeremiah 41:16).

2–6. PRAY FOR US: The remnant in Judah asked Jeremiah to pray to God and find His will on what they should do. They promised to obey (see verse 6).

7–12. AFTER TEN DAYS: After ten days of prayer, Jeremiah reported God's word, telling them to remain in the land under God's protection (see verse 10).

10. I RELENT: By this, God meant, "I am satisfied with the punishment inflicted if you do not add new offenses."

13–19. DISOBEYING . . . THE LORD: The prophet gave explicit warning not to go to Egypt, where they would be exposed to corrupting paganism.

20. YOU WERE HYPOCRITES IN YOUR HEARTS: Those who already desired to be in Egypt were hypocrites.

> *JEREMIAH TAKEN TO EGYPT: The incorrigible, disobedient leaders accused Jeremiah of deceit and forced him and the remnant to go to Egypt, despite the fact that all his prophecies about Babylon had come to pass. In so doing, they went out of God's protection into His judgment, as do all who are disobedient to His Word.*

43:3, 6. BARUCH: The faithful recorder of chapter 36 was still with Jeremiah, kept safe as God had promised at least twenty years earlier (see Jeremiah 45:5).

7. TAHPANHES: A location in the eastern delta region of Egypt.

9–13. TAKE LARGE STONES: Stones, placed in the mortar of the brick pavement in the courtyard entrance of the pharaoh's house, signaled the place where the conquering king of Babylon would bring devastation on Egypt and establish his throne. This was fulfilled in an invasion c. 568/567 BC.

12. AS A SHEPHERD PUTS ON HIS GARMENT: A simple and easy task describes how quickly and easily Nebuchadnezzar will conquer Egypt.

13. SACRED PILLARS OF BETH SHEMESH: Hebrew "house of the sun." This refers to a temple for the worship of the sun. Located north of Memphis, east of the Nile River, these pillars were said to be sixty to one hundred feet high.

44:1. THE WORD THAT CAME: The unrelenting iniquity of the Jews called for yet another prophecy of judgment on them in Egypt.

2–6. YOU HAVE SEEN ALL THE CALAMITY: The prophet summarized what had occurred in Judah as a basis for what he predicted would be coming upon the refugees in Egypt.

7–10. WHY DO YOU COMMIT THIS GREAT EVIL: Incredibly, after being spared death in Judah, they pursued death by their idolatrous sin in Egypt.

11–14. I WILL SET MY FACE AGAINST YOU: Ironically, the Jews taken to Babylon were weaned from idolatry and restored to their land; those who went to Egypt and continued their obstinate idolatry perished there.

14. EXCEPT THOSE WHO ESCAPE: A small number (see verse 28) who fled before the arrival of the Babylonian army were spared.

15. WIVES: The idolatry apparently began with the women.

17–19. QUEEN OF HEAVEN: See note on Jeremiah 7:18. This is a title sometimes erroneously attributed to Mary, the mother of Jesus, in a blending of Christianity with paganism. The Jews' twisted thinking credited the idol with the prosperity of pre-captivity Judah, further mocking the goodness of God.

20–23. THEN JEREMIAH SPOKE: Jeremiah set the record straight, saying the idol was not the source of their prosperity but was the cause of their calamity.

24–28. HEAR THE WORD OF THE LORD: Jeremiah repeated the doom stated in verses 11–14.

29–30. SIGN: The "sign" of punishment was described in verse 30 as the strangulation of Pharaoh Hophra in 570 BC by Amasis, which paved the way for Nebuchadnezzar's invasion in the twenty-third year of his reign (568/567 BC).

45:1. FOURTH YEAR OF JEHOIAKIM: The year was 605 BC (chapter 36), when the recording of God's messages to Jeremiah was in view.

3. WOE IS ME NOW: Baruch felt anxious as his own cherished plans of a bright future were apparently dashed; even death became a darkening peril (see verse 5). Possibly, he was confused by God's role in carrying through with such calamity (see verse 4). Jeremiah spoke to encourage him (verse 1).

4. SAY TO HIM: God would judge the entire nation (the Jews).

5. YOU SEEK GREAT THINGS: Baruch set his expectations far too high, and this made the disasters hard to bear. He was to be content just to live. Jeremiah, who once also complained, learned by his own suffering to encourage complainers.

JUDGMENT AGAINST EGYPT: Jeremiah had already proclaimed that all the nations at some time were to "drink the cup" of God's wrath (see 25:15–26). In chapters 46–51, God selected certain nations and forecast their doom, beginning with a prophecy against the nation of Egypt to the southwest of Judah.

46:1. AGAINST THE NATIONS: These prophecies, likely given to Jeremiah at different times, were collected according to the nations, not the chronology.

2. AGAINST EGYPT: See Isaiah 19; 20; Ezekiel 29–32. Jeremiah 46:2–12 depicts Pharaoh Necho's overthrow by the Babylonians at Carchemish by the Euphrates River in 605 BC, in which Egypt lost all its territory west of the river.

3–6. DISMAYED: Here was a derisive call to Egypt to ready itself for defeat.

10. THE DAY OF THE LORD: While this phrase often refers to an eschatological judgment on earth (as in Zephaniah 1:7; Malachi 4:5; 1 Thessalonians 5:2; 2 Peter 3:10), it also may refer to a historical day. In this case, it refers to the Egyptian defeat (see Lamentations 2:22).

11. GILEAD: See note on Jeremiah 8:20–22.

13–26. BABYLON . . . STRIKE THE LAND OF EGYPT: Babylon's invasion of Egypt, fifteen or sixteen years before the destruction of Jerusalem, is detailed here (601 BC; see verse 13). Having spent thirteen years in a siege of Tyre, Nebuchadnezzar was promised Egypt as a reward for humbling Tyre (see Ezekiel 29:17–20).

18. TABOR . . . CARMEL: As those two mountains rise above the hills of Palestine, so Nebuchadnezzar would be superior.

20–21. A VERY PRETTY HEIFER . . . FAT BULLS: Fat and untamed, ready to kill.

26. AFTERWARD: Forty years after Nebuchadnezzar's conquest of Egypt, the nation threw off the Babylonian yoke but never regained its former glory (see Ezekiel 29:11–15).

27–28. DO NOT FEAR . . . JACOB: Though Israel had been scattered to the nations, the nations would still receive their judgments, and the Lord would restore Israel (repeated from 30:10–11) from global dispersion to her own land (as in Jeremiah 23:5–8; 30–33). No matter what judgments fall on Israel, the people will not be destroyed, as Paul reiterates in Romans 11:1–2, 15, 25–27.

> JUDGMENTS AGAINST PHILISTIA AND MOAB: *Jeremiah prophesizes against the nation of Philistia, located on the coast to the west of Judah (see 47:1–7), and the nation of Moab, located on the eastern side of the Dead Sea (see 48:1–17).*

47:1–5. THE WORD OF THE LORD . . . AGAINST THE PHILISTINES: See Isaiah 14:29–32; Ezekiel 25:15–17; Amos 1:6–8; Zephaniah 2:4–7. Although Egypt's Pharaoh Hophra conquered the Philistines (who lived on the coastal plain of Palestine) in Gaza and Phoenicia around 587 BC (see Jeremiah 47:1), Babylon ("out of the north") appears to be the conqueror in this scene, at the same time as their invasion of Judah (588–586 BC; see 39:1–2).

6–7. SWORD OF THE LORD: See Judges 7:18, 20.

48:1. AGAINST MOAB: Various sites of unknown location in Moab were to be destroyed (see verses 1–5). The judgment is framed in similar words, or even some of the same words, as in other prophetic passages (see Isaiah 15:1–9; 16:6–14; 25:10–12; Ezekiel 25:8–11; Amos 2:1–3; Zephaniah 2:8–11). Desolation overtook different parts of Moab at various times, but Babylon in 588–586 BC or 582–581 BC is likely the main destroyer (see Jeremiah 48:40). The Moabites were Lot's descendants (see Genesis 19:37) who lived east of the Dead Sea and often fought with Israel.

7. CHEMOSH: This was the leading god of Moab (see Numbers 21:29; Judges 11:24; 1 Kings 11:7; 2 Kings 23:13).

10. CURSED IS HE: God's desire to judge Moab was so intense that He pronounced a curse on whatever instrument (army) He would use if they should carry it out "deceitfully"; that is, carelessly, with slackness, or being remiss (see Proverbs 10:4; Jeremiah 12:24).

11–12. HE HAS SETTLED ON HIS DREGS: This wine-making imagery is vivid. In the production of sweet wine, the juice was left in a wineskin until the sediment or dregs settled to the bottom. It was then poured into another skin until more dregs were separated. This process continued until the dregs were all removed and a pure, sweet wine obtained. Moab was not taken from suffering to suffering so that her bitter dregs would be removed through the purging of sin. Thus, the nation was settled into the thickness and bitterness of its own sin. Judgment from God was coming to smash them.

18–20. DIBON . . . AROER: These places were on the Arnon River, but would be thirsty.

24. KERIOTH: This is likely the city of Judas Iscariot. See Joshua 15:25.

25. HORN . . . IS CUT OFF: An example of the Old Testament use of "horn" as a symbol of military power, as an animal uses horns to hook, gouge, or ram. Moab was to be dehorned.

26. WALLOW IN HIS VOMIT: Here is a vivid picture of humiliation.

29. THE PRIDE OF MOAB: Suffering didn't come and humble Moab (see note on verses 11–12), so she remained proud.

47. I WILL BRING BACK: God would allow a remnant of Moab to return to the land (see 12:14–17; 46:26; 48:47; 49:6, 39) through their descendants in the messianic era ("the latter days").

UNLEASHING THE TEXT

1) What did Nebuzaradan, the Babylonian captain of the guard, say to Jeremiah that indicated he understood the judgment of God better than the leaders of Judah (see Jeremiah 40:24)?

_____

_____

_____

_____

_____

_____

2) What are some possible reasons why the residents of Judah wanted to flee to Egypt?

_____

_____

_____

_____

_____

3) How should we understand the inclusion of God's assurances to Baruch in chapter 45? How does that chapter help advance Jeremiah's message in the surrounding chapters?

_____

_____

_____

_____

4) Why do you think God had Jeremiah write down all the prophecies concerning His judgment against the nations that surrounded Judah?

_____

_____

_____

_____

EXPLORING THE MEANING

God protects His people even in times of disaster. The conquest of Judah and the destruction of Jerusalem were terrible blows for God's people. These events resulted in many deaths and ruined lives—and all because the people had refused to repent. Yet it is also true that in the midst of that disaster, God took steps to protect and care for His people. As we have seen, part of that provision extended over those who were taken captive into Babylon. Jeremiah's letter in chapter 29 reveals that the Jews in Babylon could safely work, build families, worship God, and flourish in their temporary home. Furthermore, God promised to bring them back to Jerusalem after a period of seventy years. God also provided for the remnant of His people who remained in Judah after Babylon's conquest. Speaking to that remnant through Jeremiah, God said, "If you will still remain in this land, then I will build you and not pull you down, and I will plant you and not pluck you up. For I relent concerning the disaster that I have brought upon you" (42:10). Like the captives in Babylon, God gave the Jews in Judah a chance to rebuild their lives and families—including their homes, fields, and vineyards—by extending a season of peace and prosperity over the land through the protection of Babylon's armies.

Disobedience disqualifies us from God's protection. After the destruction of Jerusalem, a large portion of the remnant moved to the region of Mizpah, north of Jerusalem. They gathered under the leadership of Gedaliah, who had been appointed by Nebuchadnezzar. Sadly, this season of respite and recovery for the people was cut short when a man named Ishmael led an insurrection and murdered Gedaliah. The people then faced a crisis: How would Nebuchadnezzar respond when he learned that his appointed leader in Judah had been assassinated? Seeking an answer, the people came before Jeremiah and begged for God's direction. "They said to Jeremiah, 'Let the LORD be a true and faithful witness between us, if we do not do according to everything which the LORD your God sends us by you" (42:5). After ten days of prayer, God's answer came to Jeremiah: stay in Judah and prosper. Specifically, God told them not to flee to Egypt: "If you wholly set your faces to enter Egypt, and go to dwell there, then it shall be that the sword which you feared shall overtake you there in the land of Egypt; the famine of which you were afraid shall follow close after you there in Egypt; and there you shall die" (verses 15–16). Incredibly, the people accused Jeremiah of lying—and then fled to Egypt! In doing so, they removed themselves from God's promise of protection.

God has authority over all nations. Jeremiah's prophecies that begin in chapter 46 declare God's judgments over many different nations and people groups. These judgments were likely not delivered at one time but collected from different eras of Jeremiah's prophetic ministry. One of the primary themes of these prophecies was that God would use Babylon to punish the evil of foreign nations—not just the people of Judah and Jerusalem. These nations included Egypt, Philistia, Moab, and others. Importantly, while Nebuchadnezzar and the Babylonian armies were the instruments of judgment, it was by God's hand and through God's authority that the judgment was carried out. "The LORD of hosts, the God of Israel, says: 'Behold, I will bring punishment on Amon of No, and Pharaoh and Egypt, with their gods and their kings" (46:25). "'A general lamentation on all the housetops of Moab, and in its streets; for I have broken Moab like a vessel in which is no pleasure,' says the LORD" (48:38).

REFLECTING ON THE TEXT

5)   When have you experienced seasons of God's protection and provision?

_____

_____

_____

_____

6) What are some steps that you can take to recognize God's provision and protection in the moment?

_____

_____

_____

_____

7) What are some of the reasons why followers of Christ often choose to disobey God even when they know what He wants them to do?

_____

_____

_____

_____

8) What are the implications of God's authority over all nations when it comes to your life today? How does that authority impact you and your choices?

_____

_____

_____

_____

PERSONAL RESPONSE

9) Think back to a recent time when you knowingly walked in a different direction than God was leading you. What were the primary reasons for that choice?

_____

_____

_____

_____

10) How will you make a better choice when you are faced with a similar situation in the future?

_____

_____

_____

_____

10

JEREMIAH'S PROPHECIES FULFILLED

Jeremiah 49:1–52:34

DRAWING NEAR
When have you recently felt tempted to say, "I told you so"? What happened next?

_____

_____

_____

_____

_____

_____

_____

_____

_____

_____

_____

_____

_____

_____

_____

THE CONTEXT
In the previous lesson, we looked at the first set of prophecies in a series of "judgments against the nations" that surrounded Judah. This list, which began in chapter 46, included the nations of Egypt, Philistia, and Moab. This list continues in chapters 49 through 51, with judgments against Ammon, Edom, Damascus,

Arabia, Elam, and Babylon. The prophesies against Babylon are especially note-worthy, as that nation was the instrument God used to judge so many other regions, including Judah. Yet Babylon was not a righteous nation; the people there committed many evils and atrocities that violated God's law and God's character. Therefore, God decreed that Babylon would also receive His judgment once He was finished using it for His purposes.

God declared ahead of time that He would use that judgment against "Babylon and against the land of the Chaldeans" (Jeremiah 50:1) as an oppor-tunity to release His people from captivity. "'In those days and in that time,' says the LORD, 'The children of Israel shall come, they and the children of Judah together; with continual weeping they shall come, and seek the LORD their God. They shall ask the way to Zion, with their faces toward it, saying, "Come and let us join ourselves to the LORD in a perpetual covenant that will not be forgotten"'" (verses 4–5).

The final chapter of Jeremiah's book takes a second (and longer) look at the fall of Jerusalem. For decades—as we have seen throughout this study—Jere-miah had preached and proclaimed God's message of judgment against that city. He declared that God would use Babylon to accomplish His judgment and that the walls and temple of Jerusalem would be torn down. Jeremiah's purpose in chapter 52 was thus to highlight the accuracy of God's message through His prophet. What God said would happen did indeed come to pass.

KEYS TO THE TEXT

Read Jeremiah 49:1–52:34, noting the key words and phrases indicated below.

> *JUDGMENTS AGAINST AMMON AND EDOM: Jeremiah prophesizes against the nation of Ammon, located to the northwest of Judah above Moab (see 47:1–7), and the nation of Edom, located to the southwest of Judah (see 48:1–17).*

49:1–6. AGAINST THE AMMONITES: See Ezekiel 25:1–7; Amos 1:13–15; Zephaniah 2:8–11. These people descended from Lot (see Genesis 19:38). Although Israel had people who were heirs to Transjordan (that is, Gad, Reuben, and one-half of Manasseh; see Joshua 22:1–9), the Ammonites, whose god was Milcham or Molech, were chided for having inhabited the area (see verse 1) when the northern kingdom was taken captive by Shalmaneser V.

2. AN ALARM OF WAR: Nebuchadnezzar defeated Ammon in the fifth year after the destruction of Jerusalem, around 582/581 BC.

4. FLOWING VALLEY: Flowing with the blood of the slain.

BACKSLIDING: See note on Jeremiah 2:19.

6. I WILL BRING BACK: As with Moab (see note on Jeremiah 48:47), God promised that captives would have an opportunity to return. This was partially fulfilled under Cyrus the Great of Persia, but will be more complete in the coming kingdom of Messiah.

7–22. AGAINST EDOM: See Isaiah 21:11–12; Ezekiel 25:12–14; Amos 1:11–12; Obadiah 1. This prophecy is closely related to the one recorded in the book of Obadiah. These people descended from Esau (see Genesis 36:1–19) and lived south of the Dead Sea. Perpetual desolation lay ahead for Edom (see verse 13), and God would make it bare (see verses 10, 18). The destroyer was probably Babylon in 588–586 BC or 582–581 BC, since verse 19 has descriptions used of Babylon against Judah (lion, 4:7; flooding of the Jordan, 12:5). Also, "fly like an eagle" (verse 22) is used of Babylon (see Habakkuk 1:8). There is no prophecy of a future restoration.

8. ESAU: He was cursed for his godlessness, and his punishment was perpetuated in his descendants (see Hebrews 12:11, 17).

9. THIEVES: Edom's attackers, by divine judgment, would not stop where normal thieves would when they have had enough. Instead, they would leave nothing (see Obadiah 1:5–6).

10. I HAVE MADE ESAU BARE . . . HE IS NO MORE: Edom was politically extinct after the Roman conquest.

11. FATHERLESS CHILDREN: This was because no adult men will be left to care for them.

12. THOSE . . . NOT TO DRINK . . . HAVE . . . DRUNK: This refers to the Jews who had a covenant relation to God. What will happen to a nation that has no such pledge?

16–17. CLEFTS OF THE ROCK: Edom, situated in high and rugged mountains, was convinced of its security and invincibility. But the ruin would come and be irreversible.

19–21. COME UP LIKE A LION: These words are repeated in Jeremiah 50:44–46, where they refer to Babylon.

20. THE LEAST OF THE FLOCK: The weakest of the Chaldeans shall drag them away captive.

> *JUDGMENTS AGAINST DAMASCUS, ARABIA, AND ELAM: Jeremiah*
> *prophesizes against the cities of Damascus, the capital of Syria*
> *(see 49:23–27); Kedar and Hazor, located in Arabia (see 49:28–33);*
> *and Elam, located 200 miles east of Babylon and west of the Tigris*
> *River (see 49:34–39).*

23–27. AGAINST DAMASCUS: See Isaiah 17:1–3; Amos 1:3–5. Hamath, a city on the Orontes River that marked the northern limit of Solomon's rule (see 2 Chronicles 8:4), 110 miles north of Damascus in southern Syria, and Arpad, 105 miles southwest of the modern Aleppo in northern Syria, were to fall in addition to Damascus. Nebuchadnezzar conquered them in 605 BC.

25. CITY OF PRAISE: This could also be translated, "the city of renown," famous because of its location in a spacious oasis and its trade, as in Ezekiel 27:18.

27. PALACES OF BEN-HADAD: Here was the place where so many cruel evils against Israel had been devised, thus the reason for its overthrow. The name is common among Syrian kings, meaning son of Hadad, an idol, so it does not refer to the Ben-Hadad of 2 Kings 13:3 and Amos 1:4.

28–33. AGAINST KEDAR . . . HAZOR: See Isaiah 21:13–17. These areas in the Arabian desert east of Judah were to be laid waste (a different Hazor was located a few miles northwest of the Sea of Galilee). Kedar was an Ishmaelite tribe (see Genesis 25:13; Ezekiel 27:21). The conqueror was Nebuchadnezzar in 599/598 BC as recounted in an ancient record, the Babylonian Chronicle. It was shortly after this that Babylon seized Jerusalem in 598/597 BC.

31. NEITHER GATES NOR BARS: These nomads were out of the way of contending powers in Asia and Africa.

34–39. AGAINST ELAM: As in Jeremiah 25:25, Elam was to be subjugated. Babylon fulfilled this in 596 BC. Later, Cyrus of Persia conquered Elam and incorporated the Elamites into the Persian forces that conquered Babylon in 539 BC. Its capital, Susa, was the residence of Darius and became the center of the Persian Empire (see Nehemiah 1:1; Daniel 8:2).

34. REIGN OF ZEDEKIAH: Jeremiah speaks of this judgment in 597 BC.

35. BREAK THE BOW: Elamites were famous archers (see Isaiah 22:6).

39. I WILL BRING BACK: As with certain other peoples in this region of nations, God would allow the Elamites to return to their homeland. In Acts 2:9, Elamites were among the group present at the Pentecost event. This has eschatological implications as well.

*JUDGMENT AGAINST BABYLON: Jeremiah's final prophecy against
the nations concerns the mighty empire of Babylon (see 50:1–51:64),
which had conquered Judah.*

50:1. AGAINST BABYLON: Babylon is the subject of chapters 50 and 51 (see Isaiah 13:1–14:23; Habakkuk 2:6–17). Judgment focuses on Medo-Persia's conquest of Babylon in 539 BC. The prediction of violent overthrow, which was not the case when Cyrus conquered Babylon (there was not even a battle), points to a greater fulfillment near the coming of Messiah in glory when those events more fully satisfy this description (see Revelation 17; 18).

2. IDOLS: The idols of Babylon are here discredited by Jeremiah's use of an unusual word for idols, meaning "dung pellets" in Hebrew.

3. NO ONE SHALL DWELL: The far view (see note on verse 1) sees this as not yet fulfilled in a sudden way. Medo-Persia came down from the north in 539 BC to conquer Babylon, but armies in the years that followed only gradually brought the historical Babylon to complete desolation (see verses 12–13).

4–10. CHILDREN OF ISRAEL SHALL COME: Jeremiah predicted a return for exiled Israel and Judah (see verses 17–20; see also chapters 30–33) as the scattered and penitent people were given opportunity to escape Babylon's doom and return to Jerusalem and the Lord in an eternal covenant (see verse 5).

5. IN A PERPETUAL COVENANT: This is the New Covenant, which is summarized in Jeremiah 31:31.

11–16. THE VENGEANCE OF THE LORD: Judgment on Babylon represents the vengeance of God (see verse 15) poured out for her treatment of His people.

17–20. ISRAEL IS LIKE SCATTERED SHEEP: This section summarizes the divine interpretation of Israel's history: (1) suffering and judgment on her (verse 17); (2) judgment on those who afflicted Israel (verse 18); (3) her return in peace and plenty (verse 19); and (4) the pardon of her iniquity under Messiah (verse 20).

21. MERATHAIM . . . PEKOD: This is a dramatic play on words emphasizing cause and effect. The first means "double rebel-lion" and named a region in southern Babylon near the Persian Gulf. The latter, meaning "punishment," was also in southern Babylon on the east bank of the Tigris River.

23. HAMMER OF THE WHOLE EARTH: This describes Babylon's former, conquering force, but God broke the "hammer" He had once used. The fact that God used Babylon as His executioner was no commendation of that nation (see Habakkuk 1:6–7).

28. VENGEANCE OF HIS TEMPLE: This refers to the Babylonians burning the temple in the destruction of Jerusalem (see Jeremiah 51:11).

29. REPAY HER: God aimed to bless Israel and curse all who cursed her (see Genesis 12:1–3, the Abrahamic covenant). The judgment on Babylon, as in Habakkuk 2, was a divine curse in view of Babylon's wrongs (see Jeremiah 50:34; 51:36, 56), particularly God's vengeance on Babylon's arrogance ("proud against the LORD"; see verses 31–32).

34. REDEEMER: The Old Testament concept of kinsman-redeemer included the protection of a relative's person and property, the avenging of a relative's murder, the purchase of former property, and even the marriage of his widow (see Leviticus 25:25; Numbers 35:21; Ruth 4:4).

35–38. SWORD: The "sword" is mentioned five times here (see Ezekiel 21).

40. AS GOD OVERTHREW SODOM: See Jeremiah 50:1. What befell Sodom (see Genesis 19) was sudden and total destruction, not like the Medo-Persian takeover but like the future devastation that will overtake the final Babylon (see Revelation 17; 18).

41. FROM THE NORTH: Medo-Persia in 539 BC.

41–46. A GREAT NATION . . . A LION: See Jeremiah 6:22–24; 49:19–21. The "lion" is Cyrus.

51:1–4. THE DAY OF DOOM: The coming of the northern invader is in view.

5. ISRAEL IS NOT FORSAKEN: Here is a reminder that God will not utterly forget or destroy His people (see Romans 11:1–2, 29).

8. SUDDENLY FALLEN: The focus is first on Babylon's sudden fall on one night in 539 BC (see Daniel 5:30). The far view looks at the destruction of the final Babylon near the Second Advent, when it will be sudden (see Revelation 18).

11. KINGS OF THE MEDES: The aggressor is here specifically identified (see verse 28) as the leader of the Medes, assisted by Persia (539 BC).

15–19. HE HAS MADE THE EARTH: God's almighty power and wisdom in creation are evidences of His superiority to all idols (see verses 17–18), who, along with their worshipers, will all be destroyed by His mighty power (see verses 15–16, 19), as in Babylon's case.

20–23. YOU ARE MY BATTLE-AX: Cyrus of Persia was God's war club. Here, the phrase "with you" is repeated ten times.

25. DESTROYING MOUNTAIN: Though Babylon existed on a plain, this phrase was meant to portray Babylon's looming greatness and power in devastating nations (see 50:23).

A BURNT MOUNTAIN: Babylon will be like a volcano that is extinct, never to be rebuilt (see verse 26).

27. ARARAT, MINNI, AND ASHKENAZ: The people north of Babylon who were conquered by the Medes early in the sixth century BC are listed here. They assisted the Medes against Babylon.

31. TO SHOW THE KING OF BABYLON: Couriers brought the report of the city's fall. Since Belshazzar was killed in the city on the night of the fall (see Daniel 5:30), this reference most likely refers to runners delivering the news to his co-ruler, Nabonidus, who was away from Babylon at the time.

32. THE REEDS THEY HAVE BURNED WITH FIRE: The method of capturing the city was to block off the Euphrates River, dry up the river bed under the city wall, and then march in. The "fire" was set to frighten the people, as it actually did.

39. DRUNK: The allusion is possibly to Belshazzar's drunken feast, recorded in Daniel 5:1–4 (see also Jeremiah 51:57).

41. SHESHACH IS TAKEN: This is another name for Babylon (see Jeremiah 25:26).

45–50. MY PEOPLE, GO OUT: Again the Lord's people were warned to flee.

58. LABOR IN VAIN: People from many nations enslaved in Babylon had built the wall, which proved useless.

59. SERAIAH . . . THE QUARTERMASTER: This man looked after the comfort of the king. He may have been the brother of Baruch, Jeremiah's secretary (see Jeremiah 32:12).

60–63. JEREMIAH SAID TO SERAIAH: This royal official carried the scroll (verse 60) to read (verse 61) in Babylon and then dramatically illustrated the coming destruction.

THE FALL OF JERUSALEM REVIEWED: This chapter is almost identical to 2 Kings 24:18–25:30 and is a historical supplement detailing Jerusalem's fall.

52:1. ZEKEKIAH: This final chapter in Jeremiah fittingly opens with her last king and his sin (597–586 BC). The purpose of this chapter is to show how accurate Jeremiah's prophecies were concerning Jerusalem and Judah.

JEREMIAH OF LIBNAH: A different man from the author (see Jeremiah 1:1).

4–11. NOW IT CAME TO PASS: See note on Jeremiah 34:1. This narrative rehearses the account of the fall of Jerusalem. So crucial was this event that the Old

Testament records it four times (here and also in Jeremiah 39:1–14; 2 Kings 25; 2 Chronicles 36:11–21).

4. NINTH YEAR . . . TENTH MONTH: For verses 4–6, see notes on Jeremiah 34:1; 39:1–2.

12. TENTH DAY: The parallel phrase in 2 Kings 25:8 reads "seventh day." Nebuzaradan, "captain of the guard" (verse 12), started from Riblah on the seventh day and arrived in Jerusalem on the tenth day.

NINETEENTH YEAR: 586 BC.

18–19. THEY ALSO TOOK: The conquerors plundered the magnificent Solomonic temple and took the articles to Babylon. A description of these articles appears in 1 Kings 6–8. Later, Belshazzar would use some of these at his immoral banquet, gloating over the victory he attributed to his gods (see Daniel 5; 1:2).

22. FIVE: The parallel phrase in 2 Kings 25:17 reads "three." There may have been two parts to the capitals, the lower part of two cubits and the upper part, carved ornately, of three cubits. The lower may be omitted in 2 Kings 25:17 as belonging to the shaft of the pillar.

24–27. CAPTAIN OF THE GUARD TOOK: Babylon executed some Judean leaders as an act of power, from resentment over the eighteen-month resistance (see Jeremiah 52:4–6), and to intimidate the nation to prevent future plots.

25. SEVEN: The parallel phrase in 2 Kings 25:19 reads "five." Perhaps these five were a part of the group of seven mentioned here.

28–30. CARRIED AWAY: The stages of deportation to Babylon include: (1) in 605 BC, under Jehoiakim, which marked the beginning of the seventy years of exile; (2) in 597 BC, under Jehoiachin; (3) in 586 BC, under Zedekiah; and (4) a mopping-up campaign in 582–581 BC. The number deported may include only males.

31–34. CAPTIVITY OF JEHOIACHIN: Jehoiachin, a captive since 597 BC, appears here in 561 BC, after Nebuchadnezzar's death, when Evil-Merodach ruled Babylon. Though detained, the former king was freed to enjoy previously denied privileges. The Lord did not forget the Davidic line, even in exile.

31. TWENTY-FIFTH: The parallel account in 2 Kings 25:27 reads "twenty-seventh." Probably the decree was on the twenty-fifth day and carried out on the twenty-seventh.

UNLEASHING THE TEXT

1) The Ammonites had inhabited the area of the Transjordan, which had been given to God's people, when King Shalmaneser V of Assyria conquered the

northern kingdom of Israel. How did God call out that transgression (see Jeremiah 49:1–6)?

_____

_____

_____

_____

_____

_____

2) What promise did the Lord make about the captives of Ammon and Elam (see 49:6, 39)?

_____

_____

_____

_____

_____

3) Jeremiah 50 and 51 reveal God's judgment against the nation of Babylon. What were God's reasons for bringing that judgment against a nation that He used to judge others?

_____

_____

_____

_____

_____

4) Jeremiah 52 focuses on the destruction of Jerusalem but also on the fate of King Zedekiah. What can we learn by comparing Zedekiah and Jeremiah as leaders and servants of God?

_____

_____

_____

_____

_____

EXPLORING THE MEANING

We cannot hide from God's judgment. Throughout history, people have attempted to hide or flee from God's wrath. Jonah is an obvious biblical example (see Jonah 1:1–3), but this is a tendency that each of us demonstrates at times. Like young children covering their eyes so their parents can't see them, we trick ourselves into believing God is not aware of our transgressions. Like Adam and Eve, we try to hide from our sin. In the midst of Jeremiah's collection of judgments against Judah's neighbors, God made this declaration to the people of Edom: "'Your fierceness has deceived you, the pride of your heart, O you who dwell in the clefts of the rock, who hold the height of the hill! Though you make your nest as high as the eagle, I will bring you down from there,' says the LORD" (Jeremiah 49:16). The people of Edom had built their dwellings in high and rocky mountains and thus considered themselves impregnable—beyond the possibility of assault. They were wrong. God's judgment was decreed because of their sin and was carried out by the armies of Babylon. In the same way, we deceive ourselves whenever we believe we can hide our rebellion from God and escape with no consequences.

We are only a step away from God's forgiveness. As mentioned previously, not even Babylon with all its military might could avoid God's judgment. Less than fifty years after Jerusalem's destruction, Babylon itself was overthrown by the Persian Empire. God predicted that judgment through Jeremiah in chapters 50 and 51 of his prophetic record. In the middle of that prophecy, God also spoke words of encouragement to those among His chosen people who would experience captivity in Babylon. But more than just encouragement, He also spoke words of forgiveness: "'In those days and in that time,' says the LORD, 'The iniquity of Israel shall be sought, but there shall be none; and the sins of Judah, but they shall not be found; for I will pardon those whom I preserve'" (50:20). This promise of pardon foreshadowed the coming of the Messiah and the message of the gospel—and it remains true of all who follow the Messiah today. As God promised through the apostle John, "If we confess our sins, He is faithful and just to forgive us our sins and to cleanse us from all unrighteousness" (1 John 1:9).

We can rely on God's promises for our future. The final chapter of Jeremiah repeats the historical record of Jerusalem's fall. The prophet reminds his readers of the consequences of King Zedekiah's rebellion against Babylon, the subsequent destruction of Jerusalem at the hands of Nebuchadnezzar, the ransacking of the temple, and the removal of 4,600 or more inhabits of the land, who were deported to Babylon in four waves. The purpose for this detailed record was not so Jeremiah could brag that he was right. It was not an "I told you so" message to those in the city who had refused to heed his warnings. Instead, the chapter serves as an affirmation of the accuracy of God's Word as declared through His prophet. When we read Jeremiah 52, we are reminded that God's Word will *always* be proven true. Such a reminder is necessary when we consider biblical prophecies that have yet to be fulfilled—such as the return of Christ, the promise of heaven, the millennial kingdom, and more. We can believe with confidence that everything God has declared through His Word *will* come to pass.

REFLECTING ON THE TEXT

5) What are some methods people use to try and hide from God's judgment?

_____

_____

_____

_____

_____

6) How would you describe forgiveness of sin? How does it happen?

_____

_____

_____

_____

_____

7) What role should confession play in our spiritual lives as followers of Jesus?

_____

_____

_____

_____

_____

8) What are some specific prophecies or promises from God that have yet to be fulfilled? Make a list of any that come to mind.

_____

_____

_____

_____

_____

_____

_____

PERSONAL RESPONSE

9) God offers His forgiveness as a free gift, which means that you cannot earn it through "good behavior." Where in your life are you currently trying to "earn" God's favor or forgiveness?

_____

_____

_____

_____

_____

_____

_____

_____

10) Which of God's promises are especially meaningful to you right now? Why those particular promises?

_____

_____

_____

_____

_____

_____

_____

11

A Lament for God's People
Lamentations 1:1–5:22

Drawing Near

What are some songs or other works of art that produce an emotional response in you?

_____

_____

_____

_____

_____

_____

_____

_____

_____

_____

_____

_____

_____

The Context

As we have discussed, the book of Jeremiah is primarily a mix of prophetic declarations and historical information. The prophetic elements offer windows from God into what *would* happen, while the historical elements describe what *did* happen. Jeremiah's prophetic record is historical in its use of facts and information. It stands as a firsthand source for the actions of kings, conversations between individuals, military battles and alliances, outcomes of warfare (such as the destruction of Jerusalem), and the plight of the remnant who remained. The book also contains Jeremiah's spoken prophecies and prophetic acts.

However, the book of Lamentations is in a different genre. Believed to be written by Jeremiah immediately after the destruction of Jerusalem in 586 BC, the book is highly emotive in nature. Thus, the content is rooted in a historical moment, but it contains the prophet's reaction to that history rather than a description of events. For example, Jeremiah wrote these words as an expression of grief emanating from the destruction of Jerusalem: "For these things I weep; my eye, my eye overflows with water; because the comforter, who should restore my life, is far from me. My children are desolate because the enemy prevailed" (1:16).

Much like the book of Jeremiah, Lamentations focuses on God's judgment against Judah—but that judgment is immediate, having just taken place. Jeremiah is weeping over the devastation that he has just witnessed. Yet, importantly, Lamentations also includes themes of hope and the reality of God's faithfulness. "For the Lord will not cast off forever. Though He causes grief, yet He will show compassion according to the multitude of His mercies. For He does not afflict willingly, nor grieve the children of men" (3:31–33). God had kept His promise to judge Jerusalem; therefore, Jeremiah could hold on to God's promise to rebuild that city in the future.

KEYS TO THE TEXT

Read Lamentations 1:1–4:22, noting the key words and phrases indicated below.

> FIRST LAMENT: *Jerusalem, formerly "full of people" (verse 1), was now lonely. Her people mourned, being forsaken by formerly friendly nations. They were in captivity, uprooted from their land. Their temple had been violated. The multitude of sins had brought this horrific judgment from a righteous God.*

1:1. HOW LIKE A WIDOW IS SHE: Lamentations 1:1–11 vividly portrays the city like a bereft and desolate woman, as often appears in other scriptures (see Ezekiel 16; 23; Micah 4:10, 13).

A SLAVE: Judah was taken captive to serve as slaves in Babylon.

2. HER LOVERS . . . HER FRIENDS . . . THEY HAVE BECOME HER ENEMIES: This refers to the pagan nations allied to Judah and their idols, whom Judah "loved" (see Jeremiah 2:20–25). Some later joined as enemies against her (see 2 Kings 24:2, 7; Psalm 137:7).

SHE HAS NONE TO COMFORT HER: This ominous theme is mentioned four other times (verses 9, 16, 17, 21).

3. CAPTIVITY: This occurred c. 586 BC, as in Jeremiah 39; 40; 52. There had been two deportations earlier, in 605 BC and 597 BC.

4. ZION: This represents the place where Jehovah dwells, the mount on which the temple was built.

SET FEASTS: Passover, Pentecost (Feast of Weeks), and Tabernacles (see Exodus 23; Leviticus 23).

PRIESTS SIGH: These were among those left in Judah before fleeing to Egypt (see Jeremiah 43) or, possibly, exiles in Babylon who mourned from afar (see Lamentations 1:3).

5. THE MULTITUDE OF HER TRANSGRESSIONS: This was the cause of the judgment (see Jeremiah 40:3; Daniel 9:7, 16).

8. BECOME VILE: This could refer to either the vile, wretched estate of continued sin and its ruinous consequences through judgment, or to being "moved, removed," as the Septuagint and Vulgate translate it. Probably the former is correct, as befits the third and fourth lines; that is, a despised, shameful, and naked condition in contrast to her former splendor (see verse 6).

9. HER UNCLEANNESS IS IN HER SKIRTS: This is a graphic description of the flow of spiritual uncleanness reaching the bottom of her dress (see Leviticus 15:19–33).

10. ENTER HER SANCTUARY: This was true of the Ammonites and Moabites (see Deuteronomy 23:3; Nehemiah 13:1–2). If the heathen were not allowed to enter for worship, much less were they tolerated to loot and destroy. On a future day, the nations will come to worship (see Zechariah 14:16).

11. SEE, O LORD: The description of the devastated widow ends with a plea for God's mercy.

12. ALL YOU WHO PASS BY: Here was the pathetic appeal of Jerusalem for some compassion even from strangers!

13. HE HAS SENT FIRE INTO MY BONES: This emphasizes the penetrating depth of the judgment.

TURNED ME BACK: God's purpose was to bring repentance.

14. THE YOKE OF MY TRANSGRESSIONS . . . BY HIS HANDS: Once the farmer had put the yoke on the animal's neck, he would control it with the reins in his hands. So God, who has brought Jerusalem under bondage to Babylon, still controlled His people.

15. AN ASSEMBLY AGAINST ME: This is not the usual assembly for a solemn feast but the army of Babylon for destruction.

IN A WINEPRESS: This speaks of forcing blood to burst forth like juice from crushed grapes. Comparable language is used in Revelation 14:20 and 19:15 in regard to God's final wrath.

17. UNCLEAN: This refers to a menstruous woman, shamed and separated from her husband and the temple (see verses 8–9; see also Leviticus 15:19ff.).

18. THE LORD IS RIGHTEOUS . . . I REBELLED: The true sign of repentance was to justify God and condemn oneself.

21–22. BRING ON THE DAY YOU HAVE ANNOUNCED: A prayer that God will likewise bring other ungodly people into judgment, especially Babylon (see Lamentations 3:64–66; 4:21–22). Such prayers are acceptable against the enemies of God (see Psalm 109:14–15).

22. COME BEFORE YOU: See Revelation 16:19.

SECOND LAMENT: Much in this chapter depicts God's judgment. He covered the Judeans with a cloud, withdrew His hand of protection, bent His bow and killed with His arrows, and stretched out a surveyor's line to mark walls to be destroyed. Yet He will rebuild Jerusalem in the future kingdom.

2:1. THE BEAUTY OF ISRAEL: This likely refers to Mount Zion and the temple (see Psalms 48:2; 50:2; Isaiah 60:13; 64:11; Ezekiel 16:14; Daniel 11:45).

HIS FOOTSTOOL: This refers to the ark of the covenant as indicated by 1 Chronicles 28:2; Psalm 99:5; and Psalm 132:7.

2. HE HAS THROWN DOWN: The Lord had cast down the bastions of Judah's defense, as He had told Jeremiah from the outset of his ministry (see Jeremiah 1:10).

3. EVERY HORN: This serves as an emblem of power, as exemplified in animals.

6–11. HE HAS DONE VIOLENCE: Tragedy comes to everything and everyone through sin. The account mentions the temple where the Israelites came to worship (verse 6), feasts and Sabbaths (verse 6), leaders such as the king and priests (verse 6), His altar and holy places (verse 7), city walls (verse 8), the law (verse 9), and children in the family (verse 11).

7. NOISE IN THE HOUSE OF THE LORD AS ON THE DAY OF A SET FEAST: A shout of triumph in the captured temple resembled the joyous celebrations in the same place at the solemn feasts.

11–12. CHILDREN AND THE INFANTS FAINT: This description of Babylon's invasion depicts the reality of a hungry child dying in its mother's arms as a result.

14. FALSE AND DECEPTIVE VISIONS: As Jeremiah 23:16–17 indicates, these lies spoke of peace and comfort, not judgment. (See Jeremiah 23:30–40 on how such lying led to destruction.)

17. HE HAS FULFILLED HIS WORD: The enemy who gloats (in verses 15–16) should recognize that the destruction was the work of a sovereign God. This verse is the focal point of the chapter (see Jeremiah 51:12).

18. WALL OF THE DAUGHTER OF ZION: The penetrated walls of Jerusalem cried out in anguish that they had been broached by the Babylonians.

20. SEE, O LORD, AND CONSIDER: The chapter closes by placing the issue before God.

WOMEN EAT THEIR OFFSPRING: Hunger became so desperate during the eighteen-month siege that women resorted to the unbelievable—even eating their children (see Lamentations 4:10; Leviticus 26:29; Deuteronomy 28:53, 56–57; Jeremiah 19:9).

21. THE DAY OF YOUR ANGER: This describes the complete slaughter, as does 2 Chronicles 36:17.

THIRD LAMENT: Jeremiah's distress in such tragedy, as expressed in this chapter, comes from God. Even the righteous experience "the rod" of God's wrath.

3:8. HE SHUTS OUT MY PRAYER: See verse 44. God's non-response to Jeremiah's prayers was not because Jeremiah was guilty of personal sin (see Psalm 66:18); rather, it was due to Israel's perpetual sin without repentance (see Jeremiah 19:15). God's righteousness to judge that sin must pursue its course (see note on Jeremiah 7:16 and 11:14). Jeremiah, knowing that, yet prayed, wept (see verses 48–51), and longed to see repentance.

16. BROKEN MY TEETH WITH GRAVEL: This refers to the grit that often mixed with bread baked in ashes, as was common in the east (see Proverbs 20:17).

21–33. THIS I RECALL: The prophet refers to what follows as he reviewed God's character. The relentless sorrow over Judah's judgment drove Jeremiah to consider the grace, mercy, and compassion of God. The tone of his thinking here changes dramatically.

22. MERCIES: This Hebrew word, used about 250 times in the Old Testament, refers to God's gracious love. It is a comprehensive term that encompasses love, grace, mercy, goodness, forgiveness, truth, compassion, and faithfulness.

22–24. HIS COMPASSIONS FAIL NOT: As bleak as the situation of judgment had become, God's covenant loving-kindness was always present (see verses 31–32) and His incredible faithfulness always endured so that Judah would not be destroyed forever (see Malachi 3:6).

23. GREAT IS YOUR FAITHFULNESS: The bedrock of faith is the reality that God keeps all His promises according to His truthful, faithful character.

27. THE YOKE IN HIS YOUTH: This speaks of the duty from God, including disciplinary training, that Jeremiah received in his youth (see Jeremiah 1:6–7).

29. MOUTH IN THE DUST: A term that pictures submission.

30. GIVE HIS CHEEK: The Lord Jesus did this (see Isaiah 50:6; 1 Peter 2:23).

33–47. DOES NOT AFFLICT WILLINGLY: God had a just basis for judgment.

38. WOE AND WELL-BEING: This confirms God's sovereign bestowal of both judgment and blessing.

40–41. TURN BACK TO THE LORD: The solution to Judah's judgment was to repent and look to God for relief and restoration.

42. NOT PARDONED: God judged their sin righteously.

48–51. MY EYES: The summary of Jeremiah's sorrow.

52–63. MY ENEMIES: Jeremiah's description of persecution sounds much like the time when his enemies at the palace had cast him into a cistern (see verse 53; Jeremiah 38:4–6). God reassured him in answer to prayer (see Lamentations 3:57), and redeemed him (see verse 58) by sending Ebed-Melech to rescue him (see Jeremiah 38:7–13). Jeremiah pleads for justice to be rendered on those enemies (see Lamentations 3:59–63).

58. YOU HAVE REDEEMED MY LIFE: Jeremiah said this to encourage others to trust God.

64–66. REPAY THEM: This imprecatory prayer for divine vengeance would be answered in Babylon's fall (see Isaiah 46; 47; Jeremiah 50; 51; Daniel 5). It will also receive its ultimate answer at the Great White Throne judgment (see Revelation 20:11–15).

FOURTH LAMENT: This chapter details God's wrath against the people of Judah.

4:1. THE GOLD HAS BECOME DIM: The gold adornment of the temple, looted by the conquerors, lost its luster with a coating of dust from the remains.

3. NURSE THEIR YOUNG: Even worthless jackals by nature nurse their young, but, under the severities of conquest, Israelite women were unable to nurse their babies (see verse 4).

LIKE OSTRICHES: Birds that are notable for ignoring their young (see Job 39:14–16).

6. THE SIN OF SODOM: Their sin was homosexuality. The fact that the suffering of Jerusalem was prolonged, while that of even Sodom was swift, marks it as the greater punishment (see 1 Peter 4:17).

7–8. NAZIRITES: Those who were the purest, most devout (see Numbers 6), strongest, healthiest, and noblest of the people became dirty, weak, and ignoble.

10. COOKED . . . CHILDREN: See note on Lamentations 2:20.

15. GO AWAY: The people chased the false leaders away.

16. THE FACE OF THE LORD: This was symbolic of divine anger. The Jews had to face up to God.

20. THE BREATH OF OUR NOSTRILS: This was a term for God, the life-giver.

21–22 EDOM . . . LAND OF UZ: In effect God said, "Laugh all you want now; your judgment will come" (see Jeremiah 25:15–29).

FIFTH LAMENT: In this final chapter, Jeremiah prays for mercy on his people. He sums up the nation's wounds and woes, recalls the woes of specific groups, shows why God judged, and intercedes for the renewal of Israel.

5:6. THE EGYPTIANS . . . THE ASSYRIANS: The Jews sinfully submitted to unholy alliances, thus expressing trust in men for protection and goods (see Jeremiah 2:18, 36).

7. OUR FATHERS SINNED: This is a cynical proverb from Jeremiah 31:29 and Ezekiel 18:2.

8–18. SERVANTS RULE: A list of horrors that had befallen Judah follow.

16. THE CROWN HAS FALLEN FROM OUR HEAD: Israel lost its line of kings wearing the crown. The Davidic monarchy was temporarily over and will not

be resumed until Christ comes as King (see Jeremiah 23:5–8; Ezekiel 37:24–28; Revelation 19:1–21).

19. YOUR THRONE FROM GENERATION: Here is the high point of this chapter. Jeremiah was consoled by the fact that God always sits on His sovereign throne, ruling over the universe from heaven (see Psalms 45:6; 93:2; 102:12; 103:19; Daniel 4:3, 34–35).

21. TURN US BACK TO YOU: God Himself must initiate and enable any return to Him (see Psalm 80:3, 7, 19; Jeremiah 24:7; 31:18; John 6:44, 65).

RENEW OUR DAYS: The intercessions of Lamentations 5:19–22 will yet be fulfilled in the New Covenant restoration of Israel (see Jeremiah 30–33).

21–22. TURN US BACK TO YOU: This plea was not made with anger. The humble, closing prayer sought God, who can never reject His people forever, to be faithful in restoring them (see Jeremiah 31:35–37; 33:25–26). In fact, their godly sorrow over sin was the beginning of that restoration, which would be completed by turning to God in faith and obedience.

UNLEASHING THE TEXT

1) Which sections or elements of Lamentations impacted you the most?

_____

_____

_____

_____

_____

_____

_____

2) What did you learn about God's nature and character from these five chapters?

_____

_____

_____

_____

_____

_____

_____

_____

_____

3) Look again at Lamentations 3:22–27. What does Jeremiah say about God's mercy in this passage? What reasons does he provide for clinging to God in hope?

_____

_____

_____

_____

_____

4) Review Lamentations 5:7–9. What similarities do you see between the culture of Jerusalem in Jeremiah's day and what we experience as followers of Jesus today?

_____

_____

_____

_____

_____

EXPLORING THE MEANING

We must honestly assess our wrongdoing. As you read through the book of Lamentations, it is clear that Jeremiah experienced many strong emotions following the aftermath of Jerusalem's destruction. One of those emotions was grief. Another was deep sorrow. Jeremiah felt horrified at the ruin of his beloved city. At first glance, it might seem as if Jeremiah were angry with God or resentful because of Jerusalem's fall. He wrote, "The Lord was like an enemy. He has swallowed up Israel, He has swallowed up all her palaces; He has destroyed her strongholds, and has increased mourning and lamentation in the daughter of Judah" (2:5). He lamented that God had "spurned His altar" (verse 7) and "done violence to His tabernacle" (verse 6). Yet a full reading of Lamentations makes it evident that Jeremiah blamed himself and the people of Judah for the consequences of their actions—not God. "Jerusalem has sinned gravely, therefore she has become vile" (1:8). Speaking on behalf of the city, Jeremiah declared, "The LORD is righteous, for I rebelled against His commandment. Hear now, all peoples, and behold my sorrow; my virgins and my young men have gone into captivity" (verse 18).

We must honestly express our sorrow. Within the church today, there is an expectation among some Christians that being Christlike means always being happy—or, at the least, not being sad. It is easy for us to adopt this mindset and fall into the routine of "putting on a good face" even when we are experiencing a crisis or dealing with loss. Jeremiah rejected such notions. He was open and honest about the emotions he was experiencing after the fall of Jerusalem. Like David and many others before him, he expressed those emotions in ways that have resonated with readers of the Bible for thousands of years. As he wrote, "For these things I weep; my eye, my eye overflows with water; because the comforter, who should restore my life, is far from me" (1:16). The prophet even spoke of God breaking his teeth with gravel and piercing his loins with arrows and expressed his horror at the sight of witnessing children starving in the streets.

We can honestly expect restoration. But like David, Jeremiah did not allow himself to dwell exclusively on negative emotions or expressions of pain. Even in the midst of his sorrow, he recalled what he knew about God's character—His goodness, compassion, and grace. "This I recall to my mind, therefore I have hope" (3:21). Then, having recalled God's goodness, Jeremiah's hope bloomed and blossomed like a flower in the desert: "Through the LORD's mercies we are not consumed, because His compassions fail not. They are new every morning; great is Your faithfulness. 'The LORD is my portion,' says my soul, 'therefore I hope in Him!'" (verses 22–24). This hope is what enabled Jeremiah to pray for restoration at the end of his lamentation: "Turn us back to You, O LORD, and we will be restored; renew our days as of old, unless You have utterly rejected us, and are very angry with us!" (5:21–22). Because of Jesus, we know that God has not rejected us. Therefore, we can have confidence that even in the darkest of times, He plans to bring us through and welcome us into a glorious future with Him.

REFLECTING ON THE TEXT

5)   Where do you see people expressing resentment or anger toward God today?

---

6) How would you describe our culture's views on expressing negative emotions? What about the views on this among followers of Christ?

_____

_____

_____

_____

_____

7) In your experience, what are productive ways for contemplating, understanding, and expressing emotions such as grief and sorrow?

_____

_____

_____

_____

_____

8) In what ways does the gospel specifically offer hope to our society?

_____

_____

_____

_____

_____

PERSONAL RESPONSE

9) On a scale of 1 (low) to 10 (high), how comfortable do you feel in expressing negative emotions to your family? What about to people in the church?

_____

_____

_____

_____

_____

10) Where do you have the opportunity right now to empathize and relate with someone who is going through an especially difficult season in life?

_____

_____

_____

_____

_____

_____

_____

_____

_____

12

REVIEWING KEY PRINCIPLES

DRAWING NEAR

What have you found most helpful in your study of Jeremiah and Lamentations?

_____

_____

_____

_____

_____

_____

_____

_____

_____

_____

_____

_____

_____

_____

_____

_____

THE CONTEXT

Our world gives us ample opportunity to think about judgment. Much like Judah during Jeremiah's day, our culture exists in active rebellion against God and His values. Our societies are prone to violence and injustice, making an industry out of war. People surround themselves with idols of every kind, relying on every-thing *except* God for provision and deliverance. We have been warned for de-cades of the consequences of such rebellion, yet we press forward with whatever plans seem best to us. Even those who follow Jesus live within nations and soci-eties that consistently oppose God's will for their lives as individuals and God's larger plan and purposes for the world. In the words of Jeremiah, "How can you say, 'I am not polluted, I have not gone after the Baals'? See your way in the valley; know what you have done" (Jeremiah 2:23).

For that reason, it can be easy to focus on everything that is going wrong—on everything that needs to be fixed, adjusted, rebuilt, or restored. Certainly, there is value in telling the truth about those realities, just as Jeremiah did. Those in rebellion against God need to hear not only about His love but also about His judgment. But at the same time, we are also called to be ambassadors of God's king-dom who trumpet the good news of God's grace.

In the following pages, you will find a few of the major principles we have found during our study of Jeremiah and Lamentations. There are many more we do not have room to reiterate, so take time to review the earlier studies—or, better still, to meditate on the passages of Scripture we have covered. As you do, ask the Holy Spirit to give you wisdom and insight into His Word.

EXPLORING THE MEANING

God prepared Jeremiah with His message. Jeremiah's task was monumental: to confront the people of Judah with the reality of their sin and then call them to repent and return to serving the Lord. What could one man possibly say to an entire nation? How could a young man stand in front of priests and kings and speak with authority? Fortunately, Jeremiah did not have to come up with his message based on his experience, wisdom, or skill. Instead, God appointed Jeremiah as His mouthpiece, declaring His message through His prophet. "Then the LORD put forth His hand and touched my mouth, and the LORD said to me: 'Behold, I have put My words in your mouth'" (Jeremiah 1:9). This language is similar to a more vivid experience expressed by the prophet Ezekiel: "Moreover He said to me, 'Son of man, eat what you find; eat this scroll, and go, speak to the house of Israel.' So I opened my mouth, and He caused me to eat that scroll. And He said to me, 'Son of man, feed your belly, and fill your stomach with this scroll that I give you.' So I ate, and it was in my mouth like honey in sweetness" (Ezekiel 3:1–3). In both cases, God provided the message that He desired His prophets to proclaim.

The people were infatuated with idols. Another reason why the people refused to repent is because they were deeply invested in idolatry. Many of the citizens of Judah, having lost hold of their faith in God and His covenants, had turned to the false gods of surrounding nations and cultures. Baal worship was common in that region and had been a powerful snare for the kings of Israel. Many in Israel had also turned to Ashtoreth, also known as "the queen of heaven." She was held to be the wife of Baal or Molech and was connected with fertility. Pagans believed that by worshiping Ashtoreth through sex with temple prostitutes, they could increase the odds of fertility for their families and fields. Most abhorrent was the worship of Molech, the fire god. Pagan priests claimed that child sacrifice—burning babies in ritual fires—would trigger Molech to offer rewards. God specifically spoke against this practice, saying, "They have built the high places of Tophet, which is in the Valley of the Son of Hinnom, to burn their sons and their daughters in the fire, which I did not command, nor did it come into My heart" (Jeremiah 7:31).

The people were puffed up by pride. God was still willing to withhold His judgment from Judah even at such a late hour. He had sent Jeremiah to confront the people with their unrighteousness and call them back to Himself through repentance. "Say to the king and to the queen mother, 'Humble yourselves; sit down, for your rule shall collapse, the crown of your glory.' The cities of the South shall be shut up, and no one shall open them; Judah shall be carried away captive, all of it; it shall be wholly carried away captive" (Jeremiah 13:18–19). Sadly, the people did not listen. Why? One reason was pride. Jeremiah cried out to the people, "Hear and give ear: Do not be proud, for the LORD has spoken" (verse 15). But still, they refused to repent. Even God mourned the pride of His people: "But if you will not hear it, My soul will weep in secret for your pride . . . because the LORD's flock has been taken captive" (verse 17). Today, pride is still one of the core obstacles that hinders people from responding to the gospel. People who overly esteem themselves to be wise, strong, or righteous will often refuse to believe the necessity of receiving forgiveness for their sin.

The future would bring salvation. In the short term, Jeremiah declared that Jerusalem would be destroyed and its people taken away as captives into Babylon. The people's fate was sealed because of their continued rebellion against God and refusal to repent. In the long term, however, God promised a different outcome. Specifically, He promised that a day would come when Jews scattered throughout the ancient world would return and rebuild Jerusalem: "But I will gather the remnant of My flock out of all countries where I have driven them, and bring them back to their folds; and they shall be fruitful and increase" (Jeremiah 23:3). This prophecy was fulfilled within decades when Nehemiah, Ezra, and others returned from Babylon, restored the city walls, and rebuilt the temple. But God offered an even greater promise further out into the future: salvation. Jeremiah prophesied about a "Branch of righteousness" (verse 5) who would come from David's line. "In His days Judah will be saved, and Israel will dwell safely; now this is His name by which He will be called: THE LORD OUR RIGHTEOUSNESS" (verse 6). This prophecy was fulfilled in the incarnation, ministry, death, and resurrection of Jesus Christ.

God's covenant promised hope. For generations, the Jewish people had experienced their relationship with God through a series of covenants—primarily the Abrahamic Covenant (see Genesis 12:1–3), the Mosaic Covenant (see Deuteronomy 11:1–32), and the Davidic Covenant (see 2 Samuel 7:8–16). These legal measures provided the expectations for Israel's existence as God's chosen people. Imagine the shock, then, when God spoke these words through Jeremiah: "Behold, the days are coming, says the LORD, when I will make a new covenant with the house of Israel and with the house of Judah. . . . But this is the covenant that I will make with the house of Israel after those days, says the LORD: I will put My law in their minds, and write it on their hearts; and I will be their God, and they shall be My people" (Jeremiah 31:31, 33). This promise of a New Covenant was ultimately fulfilled through the life and death of Jesus, as He Himself declared: "Likewise He also took the cup after supper, saying, 'This cup is the new covenant in My blood, which is shed for you'" (Luke 22:20). On the verge of destruction and disaster, God's promise of a future New Covenant was a lifeline of hope.

Disobedience disqualifies us from God's protection. After the destruction of Jerusalem, a large portion of the remnant moved to the region of Mizpah, north of Jerusalem. They gathered under the leadership of Gedaliah, who had been appointed by Nebuchadnezzar. Sadly, this season of respite and recovery for the people was cut short when a man named Ishmael led an insurrection and murdered Gedaliah. The people then faced a crisis: How would Nebuchadnezzar respond when he learned that his appointed leader in Judah had been assassinated?

Seeking an answer, the people came before Jeremiah and begged for God's direction. "They said to Jeremiah, 'Let the LORD be a true and faithful witness between us, if we do not do according to everything which the LORD your God sends us by you" (Jeremiah 42:5). After ten days of prayer, God's answer came to Jeremiah: stay in Judah and prosper. Specifically, God told them not to flee to Egypt: "If you wholly set your faces to enter Egypt, and go to dwell there, then it shall be that the sword which you feared shall overtake you there in the land of Egypt; the famine of which you were afraid shall follow close after you there in Egypt; and there you shall die" (verses 15–16). Incredibly, the people accused Jeremiah of lying—and then fled to Egypt! In doing so, they removed themselves from God's promise of protection.

We are only a step away from God's forgiveness. Not even Babylon with all its military might could avoid God's judgment. Less than fifty years after Jerusalem's destruction, Babylon itself was overthrown by the Persian Empire. God predicted that judgment through Jeremiah in chapters 50 and 51 of his prophetic record. In the middle of that prophecy, God also spoke words of encouragement to those among His chosen people who would experience captivity in Babylon. But more than just encouragement, He also spoke words of forgiveness: "'In those days and in that time,' says the LORD, 'The iniquity of Israel shall be sought, but there shall be none; and the sins of Judah, but they shall not be found; for I will pardon those whom I preserve'" (50:20). This promise of pardon foreshadowed the coming of the Messiah and the message of the gospel—and it remains true of all who follow the Messiah today. As God promised through the apostle John, "If we confess our sins, He is faithful and just to forgive us our sins and to cleanse us from all unrighteousness" (1 John 1:9).

We must honestly express our sorrow. Within the church today, there is an expectation among some Christians that being Christlike means always being happy—or, at the least, not being sad. It is easy for us to adopt this mindset and fall into the routine of "putting on a good face" even when we are experiencing a crisis or dealing with loss. Jeremiah rejected such notions. He was open and honest about the emotions he was experiencing after the fall of Jerusalem. Like David and many others before him, he expressed those emotions in ways that have resonated with readers of the Bible for thousands of years. As he wrote, "For these things I weep; my eye, my eye overflows with water, because the comforter, who should restore my life, is far from me" (Lamentations 1:16). The prophet even spoke of God breaking his teeth with gravel and piercing his loins with arrows and expressed his horror at the sight of witnessing children starving in the streets.

Unleashing the Text

1) When have you felt convicted during this study? What in particular convicted you?

_____

_____

_____

_____

_____

2) What are some unanswered questions you would like to research or discuss more after concluding this study?

_____

_____

_____

_____

3) How has your study of Jeremiah and Lamentations added to your understanding of God's judgment? How has it added to your understanding of His grace?

_____

_____

_____

_____

4) Where do you see major similarities between your community or culture and that of Jerusalem in the years before 586 BC?

_____

_____

_____

_____

PERSONAL RESPONSE

5) In what ways have you personally experienced God's judgment or correction in your life?

_____

_____

_____

_____

_____

_____

6) In what ways have you experienced God's grace?

_____

_____

_____

_____

7) What have you learned about God's nature and character throughout this resource?

_____

_____

_____

_____

_____

8) Where do you see an opportunity to stand for truth in your community, as Jeremiah did in his culture?

_____

_____

_____

_____

If you would like to continue in your study of the Old Testament, read the next title in this series: _Ezekiel: Redemption for God's People._

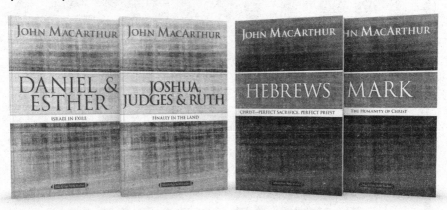

From the Publisher

GREAT STUDIES

ARE EVEN BETTER WHEN THEY'RE SHARED!

Help others find this study

- Post a review at your favorite online bookseller

- Post a picture on a social media account and share why you enjoyed it

- Send a note to a friend who would also love it—or better yet, go through it with them!

Thanks for helping others grow their faith!